NURTURING CHILDREN'S RELIGIOUS IMAGINATION

The Challenge of Primary Religious Education Today

ted by Raymond Topley and Gareth Byrne

First published 2004 by
Veritas Publications
7/8 Lower Abbey Street
Dublin 1
Ireland
Email publications@veritas.ie
Website www.veritas.ie

ISBN 1 85390 778 2

A catalogue record for this book is available from the British Library.

Designed by Colette Dower
Printed in the Republic of Ireland by Criterion, Dublin

Cover painting, 'Claude dessinant, Francoise et Paloma' by Pablo
Picasso © Succession Picasso / DACS 2004; used with permission.

*Veritas books are printed on paper made from the wood pulp of managed
forests. For every tree felled, at least one tree is planted, thereby renewing
natural resources.*

For May
the first and best of teachers

CONTENTS

CONTRIBUTORS

Maura Boyle-McNally is principal of a three-teacher primary school in Carlow. She has also served on the Religious Education Committee of the Diocese of Kildare and Leighlin and on the North Carlow Branch of the INTO. Since completing her masters she has spoken at in-service courses for teachers on the topic of Celtic Spirituality.

Peg Caverley is deputy principal/teacher at St Anne's Special National School Roscrea, Co. Tipperary. In recent years she has organised and co-ordinated summer courses on various aspects of primary school religious education.

Joe Collins is a priest of the Diocese of Cashel and Emly. Currently he is Diocesan Adviser for Religious Education. He also lectures in Religious Studies in St Patrick's College, Thurles.

Michael Hayes is an inspector with the Department of Education and Science. Prior to that he was a teaching principal. He has worked in city and rural schools, both as a mainstream class teacher and as a learning support teacher. He has also been involved as a tutor for Navan Education Centre, specialising in the delivery of courses on the use of ICT in Special Education.

Mícheál Kilcrann is a Diocesan Adviser for Religious Education in Primary Schools of the Diocese of Dublin. He co-authored *Lift Off – Introducing Human Rights Education within The Primary Curriculum* as part of the Cross Border Primary Human Rights Education Initiative 2001. In 1997 he participated in a voluntary primary school teaching programme in Uganda.

Rose Lynch is a learning support teacher. She participated in a one-year full-time pastoral course at Mount Oliver Institute, Dundalk and is trained in counselling and spiritual direction. She is a member of the Holistic Association of Ireland.

Pádraig Mac Gearailt is principal at Holy Spirit Boys' National School, Ballymun. He worked previously as a mainstream and learning support teacher. As part of the Anglo-Irish Agreement his school was involved in an East-West Project with schools in Britain. This later evolved into the Comenius Project entailing a linking up with schools in Austria and Holland.

Neasa Ní Argadáin currently lectures in Religious Education in Mary Immaculate College, Limerick. She is a primary school teacher and has served as a Diocesan Adviser for religious education in the Diocese of Dublin.

Martina Ní Cheallaigh teaches at St John of God School, Islandbridge, Dublin. She is keenly interested in the whole area of religion teaching and special education and is a member of SPRED, the international organisation for Special Religious Education.

Carmel Ní Shúilleabháin is a Froebel-trained mainstream primary school teacher at St Corban's Boys' Primary School, Naas. She has a particular interest in the area of children's spirituality and is a former president of Dominican Laity Ireland.

Gerry O'Connell is a teacher in Réalt na Mara Junior School in Dundalk. He has taught every primary school grade from Junior Infants to Sixth Class. He cherishes a great interest in the Jewish and Christian scriptures and is particularly curious as to the usage of the parables of Jesus in the religious education of the young.

Cora O'Farrell lectures in Religious Education in Colaiste Mhuire, Marino Institute of Education. She has been involved in the in-career development of teachers in the areas of School, Culture and Ethos; Personal Development of Teachers; School Development Planning; Substance Misuse. She is a member of the Executive Committee of Edmund Rice Camps.

Brendan O'Reilly is Administrator of the Veritas *Alive-O* project. Prior to that he was a primary religious education adviser for the Diocese of Dublin. He has taught in both primary and secondary schools and has been a part-time lecturer in colleges of education, seminaries and dioceses throughout Ireland. He is particularly interested in creative methodologies in primary catechetics.

Carmel Scanlon is a Froebel-trained primary school teacher with a particular interest in the spirituality of teachers. She has previously authored a booklet on Confirmation for Irish Messenger Publications.

Orla Marie Walsh is a post-primary Diocesan Adviser for the Diocese of Dublin. She is a regular facilitator and coordinator of in-service training and cluster workshops for religious educators and chaplains. In 2001–2003 she coordinated 'They Who Sing Pray Twice', a prayer initiative through the medium of music, mime and dance.

ACKNOWLEDGEMENTS

Each of the contributors to this collection of articles is deserving of a sincere 'Thank You'. On completion of their Masters studies, every one of the fifteen writers warmly and generously responded to the invitation to contribute an article based on their studies and research. In so doing they have made a significant contribution to the literature on the theory and practice of primary religious education. For this we are all in their debt.

The editors also wish to extend thanks to fellow members of the Masters in Religious Education (Primary) Programme Board: Carol Barry, Eoin Cassidy, Anne Hession, Breandán Leahy, Joe McCann, and to numerous colleagues in the Mater Dei Institute of Education and St Patrick's College, Drumcondra, who assisted in this undertaking.

The production and promotion of this volume has been supported by the Research Committee of St Patrick's College, Drumcondra, and by the Mater Dei Institute of Education, Dublin.

PREFACE

Maura Hyland

Veritas warmly welcomes the publication of *Nurturing Children's Religious Imagination: The Challenge of Primary Religious Education Today.* This book comprises a compilation of articles on primary religious education written by post-graduate students of St Patrick's College, Drumcondra and the Mater Dei Institute of Education. The majority of the writers belong, however, to the first cohort of graduates of the Masters in Religious Education (Primary) which is a programme jointly offered by the two institutes. Veritas has a particular interest in this programme, since it was at its instigation some years back that discussions first took place about the desirability of such a programme of studies being available for primary teachers.

Based on our experience in Veritas of working on the preparation and publication of programmes and resources in religious education, it seemed that an opportunity needed to be created for teachers, who had a special interest in the area of religious education, to engage in further studies which would focus, in a particular way, on the primary school. Such a programme was perceived as enhancing confidence, developing research skills, and widening the pool of expertise in this key area. It was also felt that such a programme would greatly improve the status of primary-level religious education as a discipline in its own right. Now that the first students have graduated, it is more than fitting that Veritas should publish the results of their scholarship.

While there is general agreement that the work of religious education is ideally a work of partnership between the home, the school and the parish, it is clear that, in the current context, in Ireland, the work that is undertaken and accomplished by primary teachers in this field is invaluable. In a context where religious education is becoming ever more difficult, many teachers still bring to the work a professionalism, enthusiasm and commitment which would be very difficult to replace. However, in order for it to continue, support is needed. In the first instance support from the local church community is essential. Initiatives such as relevant post-graduate programmes, which enhance a teacher's sense of competence, also ensure much needed support. Both Mater Dei and St Patrick's College are to be congratulated on the professionalism and expertise which they bring to this task. As Director of Veritas it gives me much personal pleasure to endorse this initiative. I wish those involved in the planning and coordination of the programme an abundance of imagination, energy and enthusiasm in making it a truly worthwhile experience.

Maura Hyland
Director
Veritas Publications
July 2004

OPENING WORD

CHANGE, CHALLENGE, CONCERN:

Issues in Primary Religious Education in Twenty-First Century Ireland

Raymond Topley

Change

Just as in the case of the natural seasons, change will always be an ever-present fact of human life and existence. People respond to change in a variety of ways. Some bury their heads in the sand and don't want to know. They choose to ignore change. Others are caught in a pool of nostalgia and don't wish to emerge from it. They resist change. Finally, there are those others who embrace change welcoming its challenge as an opportunity for personal and communal growth and development. For them the words of Cardinal Newman echo true: 'To live is to change, and to be perfect is to change often.'[1]

Like all other facets of life, education too is subject to change. In the past decades the rate of change in primary education has speeded up enormously. From a content approach to education, emanating from the nineteenth century and before, there has been a remarkable shift in the direction of a child-centred curriculum. Alongside this evolution one may also place developments:

- In the management of education – instanced in the establishment and operation of management boards and the various layers and posts of responsibilities willingly undertaken by various members of school staffs

- In the social organisation of education – instanced in the integration of children with special needs into mainstream classrooms
- In the substantial growth in new subject areas – instanced in the contents of the new *Primary School Curriculum* of 1999
- In the scope of and the approach to teaching the traditional subject areas – instanced in contemporary textbooks on any one of the said subjects
- In the technology of education itself – instanced in the proliferation of audio-visual equipment, and computer hardware and software in schools throughout the length and breadth of the land.

As with every other subject taught in primary schools, religious education has been affected by new thinking and has not been immune to the winds of change. At one level, changes in religious education may be understood as mirroring changes in education generally. The shift from content-centred to child-centred teaching in general education also has its parallels in religious education.

In the nineteenth century, and for much of the twentieth century, the emphasis was clearly on knowledge of religion. Catechism teaching was the order of the day and memorisation was the key to successful learning in the religion class. The years preceding and following the Second Vatican Council in the early 1960s witnessed an attitudinal change followed, in time, by a practical change. A content-focused catechesis was replaced initially by a person-centred approach. However, the person in question was not in fact the person of the pupil, but the person of Christ. This approach to religion teaching known as the 'kerygmatic approach', from the Greek term 'to proclaim', placed Christ firmly at the centre. However, this approach did not enjoy anything like the longevity of the doctrinal approach, the term used to describe question and answer catechesis, based on the teaching of the Church. Laudable as it was to highlight the role of Christ, the reality was that something else was needed to capture the imagination and attention of contemporary children, at least in the initial stages of teaching. That additional extra was human experience. And so, in the evolution of modern catechetics, what became known as the 'experiential approach' replaced the kerygmatic approach. Experiential catechesis endeavoured to take human experience seriously and to place it at the heart of its methodology.

As was the case in the rest of the Catholic world, primary religious education in Ireland responded to these developments as they occurred. The *Children of God* series of catechetical textbooks appeared in the 1970s. Its definition of catechesis as,

> The communication of Christian education
> to children in their concrete situation
> with a view to fostering faith,[2]

clearly illustrated its intent to integrate the best of the three preceding approaches. Since its inception, this series of textbooks has undergone several re-presentations, the most recent being the *Alive-O* series. Each new incarnation has been an attempt to respond to the challenge of the changing circumstances in which the activity of catechesis and religious education is carried out. The *Alive-O* approach seeks to explore deeply the human experience of life in the belief that such exploration leads to a grasping of religious reality and serves as prelude to hearing and accepting the Christian story. The overall intent of the programme is 'to foster and deepen the children's faith'.[3]

The present collection of articles grows in and out of such a soil. It, too, is concerned with the question of change and with responding imaginatively and energetically to the new challenges as they occur. Written, in the main, by primary school teachers for primary school teachers and other interested parties, these articles seek to note and name some of the challenges currently facing primary religious education today. The writers, however, go beyond merely identifying such areas. They struggle with the issues and offer creative, inspiring and imaginative suggestions as to how they might be tackled and addressed. Each of these articles emanates from the hard graft of study allied to personal experience of working with children and alongside colleagues in the teaching profession. The true genesis of these articles then is to be located not in this or that course offered within the ivory tower of academe, but rather in the life experience of the teachers themselves as teachers of religion. It is the combination of practical experience, personal reflection, and rigorous research which makes each of these articles valuable and worthwhile. They can all truly be recommended as reading for anyone with an interest today in this vital and demanding area of Church life and ministry.

Concern

At the heart of all ministry is concern, concern above all for the other, for the less fortunate. Jesus set concern for the other as a hallmark of his vision of the reign of God in the world. Not only did he preach concern, he also practised it and modeled it. A classic example of such modeling is to be found in the Lucan narrative of the widowed mother from the town of Nain, who was burying her only son (see Luke 7:11-17). An analysis of this gospel incident reveals a quite interesting three-point sequence in the way Jesus responds to the situation. It may be summarised as follows:

- The Lord saw her
- He felt sorry for her
- He acted by restoring the son to life and to his mother.

One striking feature of this particular sequence is that Jesus did not automatically move from mere awareness mode to subsequent action mode. Sandwiched between the two was the affective dimension. It was heartfelt concern for the woman's predicament that prompted the specific action. A perusal of the gospels indicates that such a manner of responding to diverse situations of need was not an isolated incident. The same pattern appears in the various feedings of the multitude stories. More significant, however, is the fact that Jesus himself incorporates this threefold pattern into his own teaching. Probably the two best known of the parables of Jesus are 'The Prodigal Son' and 'The Good Samaritan'. One presents a picture of what God is like. The other details what the ideal human person ought to be like. Yet in each of these stories, the sequence of seeing, feeling, acting is pivotal. Awareness of the plight or needs of others resolves itself in corresponding and appropriate action but only arising out of and motivated by genuine concern for the other.

A similar heartfelt concern, after the fashion of Jesus, is ever characteristic of those who find themselves in Christian ministry. Over the years it has been a feature of the work of teachers to go beyond the call of duty in order to try and meet the real needs, corporal and spiritual, of those under their care. The set of articles in this collection is in keeping with this mindset and heart-set. An examination of these writings reveals an underlying concern for all children in our schools and especially for those who are less fortunate than others in any way whatsoever. The preponderance in this collection of articles, for instance, dealing with special needs, immigrants, children from broken homes, the marginalised, and the like, is ample evidence of the survival and thriving of this element of the Christian ethical tradition. However, apart from such pieces, the remaining articles, though broader in scope, also house and exhibit at their core, the quality of concern.

Articles dealing with methodological matters, the effective use of story in religious education, the re-organisation of structures relating to sacramental initiation and life, and the recovery as well as the discovery of supportive spiritualities, are rooted in the desire of the writers – who also happen to be practitioners in the field – to reach out to all in today's schools and to provide the best possible service to each and every child. All Christian change needs to be characterised by such Christian concern and this must ever be the dominant quality in meeting the constantly emerging challenges in this current generation and in subsequent generations.

Challenge

Every one of the writers of the articles in this collection, at some stage in the recent past, had to face a challenge. That challenge consisted in considering whether or not to embark upon a systematic programme of study with a view to formally enhancing their own understanding of the demands and tasks of primary religious education today. The response to this challenge entailed not only substantial reading, lecture participation, and library research, but also the preparation and production of a significant body of work in terms of essays, reports and a final thesis. The primary education teaching profession in general and the primary catechetical community in particular has been greatly enriched by their labours. The further challenge of preparing derivative articles from the various theses for diffusion in the public domain was also met by each and every one of the contributors with admirable and unflagging enthusiasm. We are all in their debt for so responding.

The fifteen articles in this collection address a wide variety of issues. The writers were given the freedom to select a topic of their choosing. The obvious benefit so of proceeding meant that the articles were more likely to reflect the personal interests and accompanying passion and warmth of each individual contributor. The downside, however, is that some issues of contemporary importance were inevitably omitted. For instance, the issue of providing religious instruction to Catholic children who do not attend Catholic schools is not addressed. Nor is there any debate to be found in these pages concerning the place of religion in a changing and integrated primary school curriculum, nor any discussion regarding teachers who neither wish nor feel qualified to teach religion. While the topic of intercultural education is discussed, the issue of how best to service the moral, spiritual and cultural needs of non-Catholic children in a denominational school environment is not treated. The omission of these and other such topics of importance was due solely to the choices made by the individual writers. In passing, however, the importance of these additional topics is noted as is the need to address, at some time in the not-too-distant future, the particular challenges they and other similar issues present. The present volume is just the beginning of what it is hoped will be a more extended and vibrant debate on all issues relating to the religious education and faith formation of children of primary school age both in, alongside and outside of the school environs.

Change, challenge and concern will ever be the hallmark of worthwhile and creative innovation. The Irish educational system has been built upon the labour and love of many who have gone before. The articles that follow emerge from the minds, hearts and pens of yet another generation of Christian teachers intent on exhibiting a similar concern in meeting the challenge of change.

Notes

1. John Henry Newman, *An Essay on the Development of Christian Doctrine*, (London: James Toovey, 1946), p. 39.
2. M. Hyland, *Workers for the Kingdom,* the *Children of God* series (Dublin: Veritas, 1987), p. 10.
3. E.Gormally, M. Hyland and C. Maloney, *Alive-O 4* (Dublin: Veritas, 1999), p. ix.

THE CONTEXT OF
RELIGIOUS EDUCATION

CREATING SPACE FOR CHILDREN'S EXISTENTIAL CONCERNS

Carmel Ní Shúilleabháin

A four and a half year old boy called David asked me a surprising question in my fourth month as a teacher; the children had had a ten-minute 'chat time' and were free to talk to one another, draw or just listen in on the chat. David came over to where I was sorting flash cards for our next session and out of the blue he said: 'Teacher, isn't your soul yourself?' I remember it well. I was so taken aback at the profundity of the question and at the manner in which he expressed himself that it took me a little while to think what to say. I found myself loving the question and agreeing with him: 'Yes! I suppose your soul is yourself.' I wondered what had given rise to the question and where he would take it from there. David, on hearing my response took me by the hand and drew me towards his group. 'Well you better tell them because they are saying that it is not true.' The group were discussing God, your soul, heaven and hell and wanting or not wanting to go to heaven or hell. At that moment we were not in 'religion time' and we had not been discussing these issues at all. This was a great experience for me so early on in my teaching life, because it prepared me to be open to children's thinking and to expect to be happily surprised by what they might see and think and feel and say.

Children's Talk

Teachers and educationalists are fascinated by children's talk. In 1977 a team of British researchers led by Clive and Jane Erricker working on 'The Children and Worldviews Project' set out to develop a methodology that would enable them to listen to children talk about what was important to them and how they constructed meaning in their lives. The first phase of their research is set out in *The Education of the Whole Child*.[1] Analysis of the issues raised by the children in Phase 1 of the research pointed to the fundamental motif of narrative and storying across all boundaries of gender, race, age, social background and faith. To date the team has explored issues of children's social, cultural, spiritual and moral development; race and gender; emotional literacy;[2] the role of religious education and religious nurture; how children deal with death and separation; and how adults relate to children. The project is currently studying how children can become more effective learners; how children develop, spiritually, morally, socially and culturally, in respect of religious education; how educationalists and other adults might engage with children's holistic development; and finally, how adults respond to and communicate with younger people.

When Jane Erricker began this research she was very surprised by the depth of the children's thinking and by the sophistication of their arguments. Erricker believes that the reason her expectations of the children's ability to think and argue was so limited was a consequence of the influence of Piaget on her approach to children.[3]

Jean Piaget (1896-1980) was a Swiss psychologist who over a period of six decades conducted a programme of research that has profoundly affected our understanding of child development. Piaget was noted for his attention to cognitive structures, the increasing capacity of learners for knowledge, beginning with the sensory-motor level and progressing to abstract thinking. In Piaget's understanding the growth of knowledge is a progressive construction of logically embedded structures superseding one another by a process of inclusion of lower, less powerful logical elements into higher and more powerful ones right up to adulthood. Therefore, according to Piaget, children's logic and modes of thinking are initially entirely different from those of adults.

Piaget's research has had a remarkable impact on the expectations teachers have of children of any given age. The problem with Piaget's stages of cognitive development is that they focus on a certain kind of cognitive or rational knowing. Consequently his stages of development refer to cognitive development. Subsequent to Piaget's research it has become clear that there are other kinds of knowing with their own intrinsic stages of development. Lawrence Kohlberg,[4] for example, evolved a theory of moral development based on Piaget's model. Kohlberg, however, included moral knowing alongside Piaget's cognitive knowing. James Fowler's theory of faith development is also based on Piaget's structural model.[5] Fowler, however, expanded the concept of knowing to embrace the imagination and the emotional dimension of knowing. Thus the concept of knowledge being considered has evolved to include the dimensions of the 'whole person' and not simply cognitive knowledge.

Erricker found that children as young as six were capable of existential knowing and were able to base their opinions on their own life experience. They were not limited in their ability to reason and think by lack of life experience. She makes the point that children today have a great deal of life experience. What Jane Erricker discovered as key to children exceeding our expectations of their level of rational and abstract thinking was that they be given the chance. She writes: 'I don't think they were exceptional I just think I gave them the time and the opportunity.'[6]

Time is becoming a real source of pressure in teaching. There seems to be so much more to do and only the same amount of time available. So how do busy teachers give children the time they need to talk about the things that bother them and to do so in the presence of God? Experience shows it is worth taking the time to talk with children and to let them discuss issues that are important to them. There is no lack of opportunity for allowing them to express their opinions on important moral dilemmas. For example, issues that arise out of behaviour in the yard, or concerns expressed at prayer time, can be addressed later in the day.

As teachers we should never be surprised at the depth and maturity some children will show during such discussions. Erricker discovered this to be true but sounds a note of warning as to children's willingness to speak freely:

> Of course children soon become aware of what sort of discourse the teacher wishes to take place in the classroom and will not reveal such experiences [a seven year old had discussed the loss of her grandfather and how it affected her] and opinions if the ethos created is not suitable.[7]

Acknowledging Children's Existential Needs

American religious educator, Jerome Berryman, writes about the existential needs of children and how these should be acknowledged and addressed by religious educators.[8] Writing independently of Erricker, but affirming the findings of *The*

Education of the Whole Child, he describes the non-cognitive knowing that children have and relates this to his own experience as a young boy. Tucked up in bed with his grandmother, he asked her: 'Grandmother! Why do I have to die?' He does not remember her answer; he only remembers his question and her presence in the darkness. 'She put me in touch with a larger presence that seems to grow to this day.'[9] He became aware of a presence greater than himself and greater than his own questions.

Berryman discusses the struggle experienced by children when they are caught in a conflict situation described by Carole Klein as 'the double bind'.[10] This double bind occurs because of the wrong assumption made by many adults that children do not experience existential questions. This assumption leaves children with an impossible choice to make. They either deny their experience and accept the stance of adults or remain true to their experience at the risk of adult disapproval. Either way the children struggle. Berryman discusses how this double bind relates to the child's experience of the existential issues of death, aloneness, meaninglessness and the threat of freedom. Berryman finds two problems limiting the discussion on the existential concerns of children. These are the 'myth of the always happy child' and secondly a lack of evidence from literature and other sources describing how children experience existential issues.

Berryman describes his own experience with sick and dying children whom he has watched as they prepared each other and their parents for their imminent death. He observed children dealing with the existential reality of their own death and with helping others to do the same. His research affirmed that children do struggle with the meaning of life and death and other such existential issues. He has also shown how children struggling with existential issues defy the boundaries of the developmental stages set out by educational theorists. Children do struggle with life and death, separation and belonging, but they need adults to allow them the time, space and parameters to engage in the struggle in safety and with guidance.

Teaching as Presence

Berryman advocates 'teaching as presence', living the questions as opposed to wasting enormous energy denying one's existential limits. He writes of two steps required for 'teaching as presence': respect for the child's needs and knowing or understanding the questions behind their concerns.[11] Adults need to respect the religious experiences of children. He warns that the price of pretending that existential issues do not exist is to limit the possibilities of religious growth. Berryman suggests that we grow spiritually by engaging with the existential issues that belong to our human condition irrespective of age. Accordingly, religious and spiritual growth is dependent upon the acknowledgement of children's existential needs. Presence to these needs is vital for the spiritual and religious well being of the child.

To honour children is to accept each one as unique, complex and spiritual beyond our imagination. Children tempered by the limitations of not having the 'space' to be who they are and to express their existential issues may appear not to have such profound concerns as issues of life and death, loneliness and isolation. They quickly sense where and when they will be allowed to be who they are and where and when they will be allowed to express their real concerns. Given an opportunity to express themselves, however, children will far exceed our expectations.

Let The Children Speak

Robert Coles is an example of an adult who let children show him just how much they reflect on and worry about existential issues. He had studied to be a child psychiatrist, but while serving as an air force physician in Mississippi in the late 1950s he found himself in the middle of a period of serious social unrest made famous by the Ruby Bridges' story. Ruby was a seven-year-old black child who against all the odds managed to single-handedly force the desegregation of black and white school children in New Orleans. She defied all theories of education regarding developmental stages and was the catalyst for Coles becoming a 'field worker' with children from all over the world. He subsequently spent a good deal of time listening to and observing children. Eventually they confided in him. He learnt from them that children far exceed the limits set by developmental theorists, if adults give them an opportunity to speak. Coles' book *The Spiritual Life of Children* gives children a voice and in so doing encourages them to nurture and develop their spirituality.[12]

Creating a Sacred Space

The questions that begin to emerge are these: How can an ethos be created in a classroom context that allows children to share their stories? How are teachers to engage the deep existential questions of life and death, freedom, and meaning with children? The following example of how simply being present to children's needs can create for them the space necessary to work through their problems may be helpful.

Seamus, a child in my own class, was very close to his grandmother who lived in the northwest. She had been ill for some time and each morning Seamus prayed that God would make his granny better. I became concerned at his worry and spoke to his mother who was surprised that her mother's illness was affecting Seamus to such an extent. As the weeks passed and Seamus continued to pray for his granny, I realised that we had to somehow create a 'space' for Seamus where granny's healing could include God bringing her home to heaven and that this was a final healing.

An opportunity arose when we were making Mother's Day cards at art. Killian, whose mother had died, was feeling a bit sad and I chatted with him asking if he wanted to make a card for his sister who was so good to him and who had cared for him so well since the death of their mother. It was Daffodil Day that day and he had bought seven bunches of daffodils. He replied that he was bringing all the daffodils to his mother's grave. I intuitively felt that Killian was telling me something here about the Mother's Day card and so I took a risk and asked him if he would like to make a card for his mum too and bring it to her grave. His eyes lit up. Smiling he started to make his Mother's Day card. As a class we then talked about how people who have gone before us still know and love us. I spoke about my father, as that was 'safe' for the boys. I was not risking their emotions around someone they had let go to God. Seamus was listening to all of this, yet I knew that it did not yet apply to granny. Granny was going to get better.

As the weeks and days passed we talked about Easter and Christ's death, his resurrection, and the breakfast he cooked on the beach for his friends in Galilee. Seamus prayed for his granny to get better. One day I asked the boys to think about a dilemma God might have. Imagine, I said, if I was dying, and I knew that when I died I would meet God. That would be the most wonderful joy for me. I would not be in a hurry to die, and all my friends would be praying that I would get better and that God would help make me get better. What if 'better' for God, meant that God would allow me to be in heaven?

We talked about how no baby really wants to be born because it has such a comfortable place in its mother's womb. Yet look how much fun we have once we are born! I asked the boys to think about this and said that we would talk about it later in religion class. I hoped I had engaged the religious imagination of the children. Only time would tell. There was no further discussion about the matter until some three hours later. The comments from the boys were very interesting. The comments ranged from: 'Well if you were in pain I would let you die', to 'If you really wanted to I would let you die.' Responses such as the latter were a reflection on comments earlier in the day that no one really wants to die. We had a dilemma. I commented that sometimes dying is healing for the person who is dying even though it is very sad for the people who are left behind and who miss that person.

Time passed and one morning Seamus's prayer for his granny changed. He prayed that his granny would be happy in heaven. The following morning he went to see her for the weekend. He returned to school on Monday morning and prayed that his granny would be happy in heaven because she was not getting any better. That night his granny died. The boys then took over and prayed for Seamus's granny and they prayed for Seamus that he would not be too sad. We had never actually discussed Seamus and his granny. We just made space for God and Seamus to find a safe place where Seamus's prayer could change and where Seamus could accept that sometimes people do not get better, they go to heaven to God. We allowed room for that to happen, for the Transcendent to become immanent in the pain of a small nine-year-old boy and to grace him with a security about the grandmother he loved.

This story illustrates how children slowly adapt and make meaning from the existential issues in their lives providing we help them to face these issues and make meaning from them in the sacred space that we create around their pain. We need to meet children in the reality of their lives and culture and bring with us the light of God's love and care for them.

My experience of nine- to ten-year-old children leads me to the conclusion that many developmental theorists and educators writing about this age group seriously underestimate children's breadth of life experience and the depth and sincerity of the existential questions that they reflect upon and struggle with. The likes of Coles, Erricker and Berryman seem to be exceptions to this. With open minds they have taken the time to give children a voice and the opportunity to express their individuality and authentic concerns.

Notes

1. See C. Erricker, J. Erriker et al, *The Education of the Whole Child* (London: Cassell, 1997).
2. See http://www.cwvp.com/site/pubs/elbklt.html
3. See C. Erricker, J. Erriker et al, *The Education of the Whole Child*, p. 63.
4. See L. Kohlberg, *Essays on Moral Development*, Vol. 1 (San Francisco: Harper & Row, 1981).
5. See J. Fowler, *Stages of Faith: The Psychology of Human Development and the Quest for Meaning* (San Francisco: Harper and Row, 1981).
6. C. Erricker, J. Erriker et al, *The Education of the Whole Child*, p. 64.
7. C. Erricker, J. Erriker et al, *The Education of the Whole Child*, p. 13.
8. See J.W. Berryman, 'Teaching as Presence and the Existential Curriculum' in *Religious Education* 85/4 (1990), pp. 509-534.
9. J.W. Berryman, 'Teaching as Presence', p. 509.
10. See C. Klein, *The Myth of The Always Happy Child* (New York: Harper and Row, 1975).
11. See J.W. Berryman, 'Teaching as Presence', pp. 514-518.
12. See R. Coles, *The Spiritual Life of Children* (Boston: Houghton Mifflin, 1990).

CONNECTING HOME, PARISH AND SCHOOL

Cora O'Farrell

One day I was trying to coax my four-year old son to abandon his toys and join his big sister in the car so that we could set out on our weekly trip to her music class. He refused to move. 'No,' he said, 'I'm staying here!' I told him that he couldn't stay alone in the house. 'Ah, but I'm not on my own, God is with me!' he confidently replied. At this stage, time was passing, and our punctuality for the music lesson was in jeopardy. Out of exasperation I told him that God was coming with us and that he'd better come too. He chastised me for saying this and told me not to be silly – 'God is *everywhere!*'

The episode recounted above and many others like it have taken all of us by surprise from time to time and prompted many questions such as the following: From where, do our children pick up their wonderful images of God? Does it come from the home? Is it as a result of their encounter with the religion programme in school? What role does liturgy and their attendance at Mass play? How can we nurture their religious development further? What supports are available to me as a parent? The quest for an answer to these questions suggests a consideration of the three main agents responsible for the religious development of children and the manner in which these operate together.[1]

Home, Parish and School

For the child the three pillars of religious development are the family, the parish and the school. Together they form a unity, each providing a fundamental component in the Christian formation of the child. It is essential that they work in partnership with one another so that the child's religious development is nurtured to the full. It is apparent however, that in many instances, this partnership is less than perfect.

Martin Kennedy in *Islands Apart,* a consultation report on the *Children of God* series, published in the year 2000, illustrates that the religious education programme in Irish primary schools appears to be working well.[2] He confirms, however, that parishes have become places of 'diminishing religious discourse' while, in the home, the level of religious experience and discourse is also quite low. Kennedy coined the phrase 'Islands Apart' to describe the limited partnership that exists between home, school and parish. His report is a powerful one that captures well the picture as it exists today. The focus in this present article is on the home and on how the school can support both home and parish in their endeavour to nurture the religious development of young children aged three to six. It contends that those parents who are intent on nurturing the religious development of their children are in need of guidance and support and that parish and schools can and should help to provide such support. The effect of home, school and parish working in partnership should have a major influence on the religious development of young children.

The Home

The primary catalyst in the faith formation of the young child is the family. It is what happens in the home, day in and day out, which is the most important dynamic for faith formation.

Parents are the 'primary educators in the faith.'[3] They pass on human values and the Christian tradition as well as nurturing a sense of God in their children. Faith development theorists agree that very young children's sense of the Divine is related to the quality of the relationship that exists between them and their parents.

In Ireland and elsewhere, in recent decades, the notion of 'family' has changed significantly. Prior to this, the typical 'family' would have consisted of father, mother and a number of children. The father probably would have worked outside the home, as the 'bread-winner', and the mother would have remained at home. Grandparents would have maintained close contact with the family and their influence and support would have been keenly sensed. The family would have attended Mass on a weekly basis and the Church would have had a strong influence on their lives. It is no exaggeration to say that this portrait would have been characteristic of a typical Catholic family in Ireland in the fifties, the sixties and even into the seventies.

However, there have been many changes in Irish society in recent decades which have had enormous impact on the family. The increase in the number of dual working parents, both of whom spend long hours at work outside the home, has meant that the amount of time that many parents have with their children has significantly decreased. Less time with children means less parental influence while other facets of everyday life such as a surfeit of television viewing have moved in to fill the void. There are also other challenges to the quality of family life including marital break-up and family violence. The traditional notion of family with father, mother and children can no longer be assumed to be the norm. In addition, the supportive connection with grandparents has also diminished significantly in many instances.

The Parish

The parish is the local Christian community that gathers for worship and whose members serve and support each other and reach out to the wider world. For many parents, however, the parish church is no longer a focal point of contact. Attendance at church services has declined considerably and increasing number of parents have lapsed from the faith. Recent scandals relating to the Church have given rise to cynicism among many who claim that the 'witness' dimension of the Church has been obscured at best, or worse still is not in evidence at all. This cynicism is primarily directed at the credibility of some of its personnel and at some of the structures of the Church, rather than at its faith practices. Evidence of this can be seen in the overwhelming majority of parents who still present their infants for Baptism. They are typical perhaps of those who have been baptised themselves, but who lead lives divorced from the formal Church. Reawakening the faith of adults such as these, who no longer practice actively, is a real challenge for the Church today.

The *General Directory for Catechesis* highlights the need for more direct focus on adult catechesis, as without this any other catechetical enterprise will have limited success. Boston College-based religious educationalist, Tom Groome, echoes this notion by calling on the Church to 'nurture the nurturers'.[4] This can be done through the creation of networks of support among parents and by investing ministerial time in this endeavour. The primary approach adopted should be an appeal to the immediate life experiences of parents and an attempt to recognise a spiritual dimension to these immediate priorities. This is the essence of good catechesis. It starts from life experience, moves on to the sharing of the Christian story, and then reappraises life experience in light of the Christian story.[5]

Parish baptism teams are a good example of this in practice. Many parishes now have baptismal teams which comprise committed lay people. Their ministry is especially important as they connect with parents at a very special moment in their lives when they are deciding to have their child baptised. Some parishes incorporate home visitation into their baptism preparation. When this occurs it is a very effective way of expanding people's perception of parish. In this way the Church is clearly seen as referring to something beyond just a building or an institution.

The success of baptism teams is due largely to their pastoral approach. Their purpose is to evangelise parents in their role as the primary religious educators of their children, but their method is primarily that of building relationships. Baptism teams demonstrate that what many people need first and foremost is not just sermons or ritual celebrations but the mutual support of a community.[6] Changing times require changes in approach without at the same time missing out on the core of the Christian message. Francoise Darcy-Berube states the case well:

> The practice we should be concerned about in our evangelising ministry is ... openness of heart through faith and prayer to the gift of God's love, to the joy of the kingdom, which some day will bring them to the Table, because they will hunger and thirst for a deeper communion.[7]

Unfortunately in most parishes this close contact with parents is dropped a short time after the baptism of their infants. This is most regrettable as the next time most parents receive any formal support in the spiritual nurturing of their children is when they start school.

Pope John XXIII's image of parish as the 'village fountain,' where people meet while gathering life-giving water, is one worth striving towards. Recent developments illustrate how parishes have made great strides in their attempts to cater directly to the needs of young children and their parents. Innovative approaches for engaging young children in the Mass, for example, have produced liturgies which are relevant to their stage of development and level of interest. Such celebrations enable families to partake in a true celebration of the Eucharist which connects with their lives. Parish newsletters, parish groups and parish websites are other examples of means through which parishes seek to engage with their members. Much remains to be done, however. The following examples suggest creative ways of reaching out to parents which could be adopted by parishes in order to support parents in their role of nurturing the religious development of their children:

- Provision of guidance for parents regarding prayer and ritual practices with their children
- Building of relationships with parents in the home and gradually inviting them into a process of evangelisation and catechesis
- Development of structures to meet first-time parents of children in the post-Baptism pre-school stage of their development
- Empowerment and creation of leaders in the community
- Provision of ongoing formation and catechesis for those in leadership positions within the parish
- Training of personnel at pre-school level in the forms of religious education suitable for young children.

It is difficult for parish personnel to offer support to those parents who are disconnected from parish. For such parents, school becomes the best possible place where they can receive support in their role. The school, therefore, could become a focal point for the catechesis of parents during an interim phase of reconnection with the parish.

The School

Historically, in Ireland, the Catholic primary school attached to the parish has had responsibility for the task of providing for the formal religious education of children. Research has shown that religion programmes such as the *Children of God* series and, its successor, the *Alive-O* series have made an important contribution in this regard.[8] However, all too frequently the task of catechising children has been viewed as the responsibility of the school. Oftentimes, parents' responsibility in this respect has been minimised as a result. Whether this is seen as an abdication of responsibility or as empowerment may be debated. Nonetheless it has become clear that the main religious zone for catechesis of primary school children has often been the school.

The *Alive-O* programme has the capacity and resources to link home, parish and school in the task of nurturing the religious development of young children. The home/school/parish partnership is very much in evidence in *Alive-O*. Each class programme at the junior end of the school, offers three opportunities for parents and parish representatives to join the children in their classroom for prayer services celebrating the children's progress in the programme. At later stages in relation to the celebration of first Confession, first Communion and Confirmation, there are many more opportunities for linking home, school and parish indicated in the programme.

Anecdotal evidence suggests, however, that home/parish/school links at the junior end of the school are not being utilised to their full potential. There is sensitivity for example, on the part of some teachers about inviting parents to attend a prayer service during school hours. They realise that many parents may not be able to participate due to work commitments and that some pupils will be upset as a result. Creative ways of approaching such gatherings need to be explored so that important opportunities such as these are not lost.

Religious Education Co-Ordinator
The value of the religious education programme in school may be diminished without some key person being responsible for ensuring its progress and development. In the past it was the parish clergy who fulfilled this role. However, with the reduced number of priests available, it is unrealistic to expect them to have as much time to carry out this role. Diocesan Religious Education Advisers also are too few in number to make a significant impact at local level. There is a need, therefore, for a link person attached to both the parish and the school. Ideally, such a person would be a member of the parish community, teaching in the parish school. He or she could in the future, perhaps, be part-time in parish and part-time in school.

The model of the Home/School/Community Liaison Scheme (H/S/C L) Scheme, initiated by the Department of Education and Science, in 1990, is one which could be helpful in suggesting a way of progressing towards fulfilling just such a role:

The underlying philosophy of the H/S/C L Scheme is one that seeks to promote partnership between parents and teachers in order to enhance the pupil's learning opportunities and to promote their retention in the education system. This is pursued by identifying and responding to parent needs and by creating a greater awareness in teachers of the complementary skills of parents in their children's education. The scheme seeks to promote active co-operation between home, school, and relevant community agencies in the education of young people. The scheme focuses directly on the salient adults in the pupils' educational lives and seeks indirect benefits for the children themselves. In short, the H/S/C L Scheme seeks to develop the parent as prime educator.[9]

The chief resource person in the Home/School/Community Liaison Scheme is the local co-ordinator who is a teacher based in the school but relieved of teaching duties. One possible response might be the creation of a similar role in the area of religious education. The Religious Education Co-ordinator would be a teacher who, upon assumption of this new role, would be withdrawn from teaching duties. The overall aim of their work would be to assist the nurturing of young children's spirituality and faith formation. Their *modus operandi* would be that of linking with the significant adults in the child's life, namely parents or guardians and teachers. The Religious Education Co-ordinator would visit homes and connect with parents at whatever stage they are at. They would offer support, ranging from providing courses, for instance, for those who are at an advanced stage in their faith journey, to that of building a positive relationship with an isolated parent whose stress level may be wreaking havoc in their child's life. Within the school itself, the Religious Education Co-ordinator could link with the teachers in the school and seek to fulfil any catechetical training requests which might arise. They could also be involved in policy development and in ensuring that the *Alive-O* series is utilised to its full potential.

The Religious Education Co-ordinator would also be responsible for connecting with parish personnel and for sharing what is happening in the school with those who are involved in parish activities. This could include briefing a Family Mass group, for instance, on the songs which are being learned in school at that time. The efforts of everyone involved would ensure that the role of parish as a vital source of life for all – parishioners and parents, priests, teachers and children – would be fully realised.

Summary

It is in the home, the school and the parish that the religious development of young children is nurtured. When these three elements work in partnership, opportunities for children's religious development are optimised. At present, this is not the case. The home is particularly isolated with many parents distanced from their parishes. It is the school, therefore, which possesses the capacity to rekindle an effective partnership. An initiative such as the Religious Education Co-ordinator, as outlined above if implemented, could contribute in no small way to reconnecting the islands of home, school and parish which might otherwise continue to drift apart.

Notes

1. The innate spirituality of children is taken as a given here. For a consideration of this topic see E. Robinson, *The Original Vision* (Oxford: The Religious Experience Research Unit, Manchester College, 1977); R. Coles, *The Spiritual Life of Children* (Boston: Houghton Mifflin, 1990); D. Hay with R. Nye, *The Spirit of the Child* (London: Harper Collins Religious, 1998).
2. See M. Kennedy, *Islands Apart* (Dublin: Veritas, 2000).
3. Congregation for the Clergy, *General Directory for Catechesis* (Dublin: Veritas, 1998), par. 255.
4. Cited in F. Darcy-Berube, *Religious Education at a Crossroads: Moving On in the Freedom of the Spirit* (New York: Paulist Press, 1995), p. 111.
5. See T.H. Groome, *Sharing Faith: A Comprehensive Approach to Religious Education and Pastoral Ministry – The Way of Shared Praxis* (Eugene, Oregon: Wipf and Stock, 1998).
6. D. O'Donnell, 'My Hopes for My Church', *The Tablet* 15 February 2003, p. 2.
7. F. Darcy-Berube, *Religious Education at a Crossroads*, p. 92.
8. See M. Kennedy, *Islands Apart*.
9. C. Conaty, *Including All: Home, School and Community United in Education* (Dublin: Veritas, 2002), pp. 69-70.

CONTEMPORARY THEMES IN PRIMARY RELIGIOUS EDUCATION

DEVELOPING A 'CULTURE OF CARE' IN A DISADVANTAGED AREA

The Contribution of an Educational Community

Pádraig Mac Gearailt

Why am I suspending so many students and what am I suspending them to?

These two basic questions caused many sleepless nights in the early years of my principalship, nearly seventeen years ago, at Holy Spirit Boys' Primary School in the seriously disadvantaged area of Ballymun, Dublin. While studying a log of suspensions over a period of a full academic year, it became clear that while fifty-two pupils had indeed been suspended for one, two or three days duration, the actual number of boys involved was recorded in the low twenties. This fact was explained by the 'recidivist' nature of a small number of pupils. While the majority of this cohort of pupils was removed for violent and aggressive actions towards other students, a minority was sent to the principal because they were not 'co-operating' with the teacher in the classroom.

The most serious concerns arising from the act of suspending pupils related to the family background of these pupils and the inability of their parents to positively influence their child's challenging behaviour. I learned this lesson early in my tenure of office when having brought a child to his first floor flat for continuously disrupting the class, his mother, assured me that her son would be confined to his room for the remainder of the day. Before I reached the school (a walk of approximately five minutes) this boy had already managed to enter the school grounds and to break a window. He stood proudly outside the school railings informing me of his recent exploit. This sense of tension, dilemma and conflict, affecting the right of the majority of pupils to receive an education, whilst a handful of disruptive students feel that they can act out their unacceptable behaviour, has not been addressed by recent educational legislation. In fact, the inclusion of Sections 28 and 29 of the Education Act (1998) would seem to undergird the position of the tiny minority of pupils whose behaviour can cause disruption to others. The balancing of rights is complex and difficult.

This article seeks, by describing the reality of disadvantage on the ground and elaborating on efforts made at various levels, to provide a 'culture of care', to suggest the possibility, even in the most difficult of circumstances, of developing an approach to disadvantage that allows the young person to believe that new things are possible. When a secure, stable and stimulating learning environment has been achieved the themes suggested in other chapters of this book can come into their own.

The Local Environment from a Historical Perspective

On 2 June 1963, 20 Bolton Street in Dublin's inner city collapsed into the street killing Mrs May Maples and her husband John. Then, ten days later, two young girls, Linda Byrne and her friend Marie Vardy, were killed when another tenement in Fenian Street collapsed as the girls were going to the shops to buy sweets.[1]

Between the mid-1950s and the early 1960s the number of houses built by local authorities in Ireland declined. With the exception of Portugal the number of new houses built in proportion to the population was lower than in every other European country. It must be remembered that this was against a background of mass emigration from an impoverished Ireland, where the effects of the first programme for Economic Development, the brainchild of Seán Lemass and T. P. Whitaker, were just about to be noticed. Reacting to the anger of the capital city's citizens, Dublin Corporation's Housing Committee agreed that all existing housing priorities should be immediately suspended with priority status being transferred to families who had been displaced from dangerous buildings. It was estimated that 26 per cent of the housing stock in Dublin City and County had already exceeded their estimated life expectancy.[2]

The declaration of the dangerous buildings emergency in June 1963 led to nine hundred families and 326 single persons being forced to evacuate their homes. Only fifty-nine such notices had been issued prior to 1962.[3] In response to the developing housing crisis Dublin Corporation estimated that the need for approximately 10,000 dwellings existed. The National Building Agency Limited declared that, even by committing all of its available land and technical resources to a building programme, Dublin Corporation would be unable to provide for existing urgent cases for four years. However, under political pressure from Taoiseach Lemass, the Minister for Local Government, Mr Neil Blaney, met a deputation from Dublin Corporation on 19 January 1964 to consider a report on system-building. This report had arisen from a visit by senior engineers in his Department to London.[4] The Minister proposed that the site for the development of a system-built scheme of housing would be the Albert Agricultural College which was owned by University College, Dublin. In February 1964, a special meeting of University College Dublin Governing

Body approved the sale of 359 acres to Dublin Corporation. On the northern section of this site, on 212 acres, the Ballymun housing scheme was to be developed. The southern portion of 147 acres eventually became the site for the new Dublin City University. On 12 June 1964, Minister Blaney received a letter from Dublin Corporation asking him to proceed with the Ballymun project. Advertisements subsequently appeared in the Irish newspapers and later in various journals throughout Europe. With approximately three thousand dwellings to be built, interest was widespread. Eighty-nine companies responded to the advertisement, including firms from Ireland, United Kingdom and the Continent.[5] On 25 August 1964 the Government agreed that the National Building Agency would effectively manage the building programme on behalf of Dublin Corporation, the Department of Local Government and An Foras Forbatha (the National Institute for Physical Planning and Construction Research).[6]

On 13 November 1964, Minister Blaney announced that a decision had been taken to award the contract to the Cubitt Haden Sisk consortium. Sisk's had already been involved with housing in Ireland from 1949 and were the contractors for the construction of Liberty Hall, then the highest building in Dublin. The Minister signed the contract with the consortium on 2 February 1965, at a cost of £9,190,808. The degree of flexibility attached to the contract favoured the contractors who dispensed with some of the more progressive elements of the proposed planning arrangements. A major issue was the jettisoning of the substantial landscaping plans, which had helped to secure the support of the neighbouring local residents groups.[7]

Fifty years after the 1916 Rising, the building of this new town brought the hope of a brave new beginning. Despite the great expectations accompanying the project it quickly became a social and political failure. Notwithstanding the requirement in the contract that the system building methodology provide greater speed of production of housing, throughout the duration of the contract the builders consistently missed handover times. By May 1966, the first handover had still to take place.[8] On 20 December 1968, the *Irish Times* reported that the Ballymun project was officially completed. But from the outset problems emerged with the design of the buildings, with lifts breaking down and with an unreliable district heating system which could not be controlled in each flat unit. By the early 1970s there was a tenancy turnover rate of 50 per cent.[9] It would appear that the focus on speedy provision of housing had been at the cost of the human needs of the population.

This new model of an Irish town of approximately 22,000 inhabitants was promised shopping facilities, office accommodation, an entertainment centre comprising a dance hall, cinema, skating rink, restaurants, bars, community centre, meeting hall and swimming pool.[10] However, five years after the completion date, the population had been provided with only two pubs, a snack bar and a swimming pool. Fast forward three decades and little had changed. At the beginning of the new millennium, Frank McDonald described Ballymun as 'the State's worst planning disaster.'[11] The town was still dogged by a lack of the infrastructural requirements for a population in excess of twenty thousand people. The shopping centre had been allowed to deteriorate over the decades to the extent that prime units were left vacant and the locals shopped elsewhere. The curse of drugs had affected many families and was a blight on the area. In 1998 there were 683 know opiate users in the local area, two-thirds of whom were male. Also, each time Dublin Corporation opened another large local authority housing scheme, it signalled an exodus from Ballymun to Tallaght, Darndale and Finglas South. The Government decision to offer a sum of £5,000 to local authority tenants to move to private accommodation was a further factor in denuding the community of leadership potential.

A New Beginning

Out of all the aforementioned failed history was born Ballymun Regeneration Limited (BRL), a subsidiary company of Dublin Corporation, which came into being to rectify the mistakes of the previous decades. One of the great lessons learned was the necessity to engage in consultation and dialogue with the local population, as in contrast to other such projects in Europe, the residents would remain 'in situ' while the renewal of the town would progress. At a cost of 2 billion euro this would be the biggest rebirth project in Europe. BRL decided to contact the National College of Ireland to design courses on personal and community development, architecture, gardening, home maintenance, conflict resolution and change management to assist residents in their transition from high rise living to the five new neighbourhoods concept. Regular newsletters were circulated giving updates on the developments for the community.[12] A website was established containing the full masterplan for the regeneration.[13] A fundamental factor in changing the public perception of the area, in marketing terms, has been the granting of Urban Renewal Tax Incentive Status. Its proximity to the M50 and the possibility of a spur line of the Metro/Luas to Dublin Airport, passing through the town, may help to convert its image from one of 'edge city stigma'. Probably the greatest factor in changing Ballymun into a sustainable community will be the development of mixed housing in the area with a definite programme of private housing.[14] At the moment there is still an existing lack of balance in tenure at Ballymun – 80 per cent local authority rented and 20 per cent owner occupied.

The School in the Local Environment

Holy Spirit Schools opened to cater for the new children arriving into Ballymun. It was the original primary school in the area receiving its first pupils on 3 July 1967.[15] Initially it opened as a co-educational school but within fourteen months developed as separate boys and girls schools on the same campus. Pupil numbers increased rapidly and reached maximum figures in 1973 when 2,200 children attended the schools. Class sizes were exceptionally large. There was no remedial support or special classes for the weaker pupils. Corporal punishment was allowed in schools until banned by Minister for Education John Boland TD in 1982, but had never been the main feature of discipline in the school. Teacher retention was a problem over the years, until teacher mobility in Ireland was curtailed in the 1980s, when young teachers were forced to emigrate due to the Government's embargo on recruitment. Within the local community the school remained as a focal point of continuity – creating a bond between pupils, parents and their extended families. In the late 1990s between retirements and career breaks and teachers moving out of Dublin for various reasons, there was a renewal of staff, with all coming directly from the Colleges of Education. Despite the social upheavals within the community over the decades, the school had managed to cope successfully in fostering good relationships with the boys and their parents. Discipline was strict, but generally fair. It was now time to formalise a policy regarding behaviour in the school. Having studied a number of different systems of discipline, I, as principal, had been impressed by a presentation about 'Discipline for Learning' (DFL) given by its author, Adrian Smith, at a conference organised by The Southside Partnership, a government supported initiative seeking to draw together all those interested in building up and providing opportunities in south Dublin. Head teachers from various types of schools in England and Scotland spoke about the difference this system of discipline had made to their schools. It appeared to answer the main questions about keeping pupils on task by giving them choices and responsibility for their own actions. It also sought a balance between rewards and sanctions. Smith stressed the importance of projecting a positive climate by seeking two good behaviours before checking one bad behaviour.[16] He advised on the necessity to consult widely to achieve agreement on setting the rules, rewards and sanctions for the programme of discipline within a school.

The Process and The Product
After raising the issue at a staff meeting in 1996 and following a wide-ranging discussion on discipline in the school, it was agreed to set up a subcommittee to consider the approach to be taken to the introduction of our form of DFL. The Board of Management also agreed to fully support the new system. Members of the subcommittee visited a number of schools in the city and county during 1997 to ascertain how the DFL programme worked in different school settings. In each case the reports were very positive. Ballymun Partnership was approached, through its Education Officer, for funding to bring the charismatic Smith to train the teachers and members of Board of Management in this new system. He provided direction and guidance for the sub-committee in formulating our school's policy. The Board of Management agreed to close

the school for two full days to allow the training programme take place. It also committed to fund a reward system for the pupils to promote good behaviour.

The full day workshop proved to be very informative in providing a valuable space to consider our present practices. After this the Home/School/Community Liaison teacher took the lead in organising the DFL sub-committee to address the issues of differing practices by different teachers in order to encourage team players rather than solo performers and to create a collaborative approach to problem solving. This process led to the task of examining our ethos and school culture in the light of the changing character of the school. The assistance of the School Development Planning Facilitator was sought in carrying out this module of work. He emphasised that it was crucial that everybody in the school community should accept the agreed formula as a 'living' document. The following School Vision/Mission Statement was agreed:

> The school's vision is one of providing a secure, stable and stimulating learning environment in which each individual child will develop to his fullest potential intellectually, morally, physically, spiritually, socially, culturally, aesthetically and emotionally. The uniqueness of the individual person will be respected and indeed promoted through a process of nurturing and developing each child's identifiable abilities, self-esteem and talents in order to help him to progress towards realising his fullness in adult life and in society. To this end, the promotion of a strong sense of community within the school is dependent on high levels of cooperation between Board of Management, teachers and ancillary staff and local groups. The support and co-operation of

parents is encouraged. All of this goes towards providing our pupils with the very best in primary education in a caring, Christian atmosphere.

From this mission statement a 'culture of care' would come to fruition, which required a common approach by all staff. One of the main facts emerging from group sessions was that, as teachers, we do not use praise often enough. Through the Discipline for Learning system this deficit could be addressed by sending home regular notes to parents praising their children's behaviour. Also a certificate would be given to each child who achieved 150, 300 and 450 stars in their merit books. Each child is provided with a merit book at the start of a new term. In this book the teacher records the stars the child earns for positive behaviour or yellow cards for failure to follow agreed rules.

My Points for this Week						
	Uniform	Homework	Stage One	Stage Two	Stage Three	Bonus!
Monday						
Tuesday						
Wednesday						
Thursday						
Friday						
Total						
	Total points for the Week:					

In June a special medal would be presented at a prize-giving ceremony. It was agreed that the good news should be spread so public award ceremonies were held each term to acknowledge the pupils' efforts. Gradually, it became evident that 95 per cent of our pupils fully co-operated with their teachers on a daily basis, five per cent caused some problems, while 1 to 2 per cent demand an inordinate amount of attention and time. It was a surprise that such a high percentage of students were so compliant and it was important that this fact be celebrated and recognised by all. Similar figures have been found in other surveys.[17] Without a doubt, the greatest challenge for any behavioural programme is how to cope effectively with this 1 to 5 per cent of pupils. Generally, the pupils falling into this category are failing to experience success and need to be placed on individual learning programmes to give them the 'taste' of success. Our school was granted a teacher counsellor (now known as a support teacher) who supports a core group of approximately twenty pupils who are disruptive, disturbed and withdrawn.

This group of pupils is selected on the basis of consultation between the mainstream teachers, the support teacher and the principal. The support teacher works with the particular group of boys on an individual basis, in pairs, or in small groups, in order to build-up a special relationship with the pupils and to improve their self-esteem and work skills. Each post of responsibility holder mentors four pupils; meaning that the teacher will take a positive interest in these pupils, who are not in their own class group.

Over the past ten years, there have been two special learning classes in the school. Originally, the special class pupils remained with their teacher all day. Now these pupils are integrated into the mainstream classes for the wider curriculum, but receive individual programmes in reading and number in their base special class. Both special classes meet at the lunchtime each day and are treated to a hot meal. This ritual helps to strengthen the relationships between both groups, who previously felt isolated. The arrangement also helps the older pupils in the junior special learning class to become familiar with the senior special class teacher, thus easing the transition to the senior class. Over the years, it has been noticed that the younger pupils are reluctant to taste 'new' flavour foods, as they have no experience of different vegetables and fruits. The teachers try to provide the boys with different food experiences.

The senior special class teacher has introduced a collaborative learning approach into his class through the Lego Mindstorms programme, combining Lego robotics and computers. So successful has been this form of learning that the mainstream pupils clamour to be accepted into this co-operative working/problem-solving atmosphere.

The gains over the past six years for the school community in adopting the Discipline for Learning system coincide with the findings of the Martin Report on Discipline in Schools (1997):[18]

- Fewer suspensions have occurred
- Children's self-esteem has improved
- Good behaviour now being recognised and rewarded
- 95 per cent of children are capable of making informed choices
- Parents are happier receiving good news and are fully supportive of the new approach
- Children are happier in school
- Children know the consequences of their actions and choices.

In our school we have found that the merit book, which each pupil has, can also be used to monitor attendance and trace the behavioural patterns of individual pupils. The school day is divided into three sections. The first period covers from entry time until the lunch break at 11 a.m. The second period is from 11 o'clock until the yard break at 12 o'clock. The afternoon session stretches from 12.30 until departure time at 2.35 p.m. Every pupil can gain a star for each of the three periods. A bonus star can also be gained at the discretion of the teacher. An important element of this system is the 'cleaning of the slate' at the end of each session or period, so that a pupil can still gain stars and retain an incentive to behave in class. Two other areas where stars can be gained are for wearing the uniform or tracksuit and for producing homework. Previously these could be contentious 'battleground' situations, but now the pupil makes the decisions, which are recorded in their merit book. This book is a useful tool to encourage pupils to track their own behaviour. Another benefit with the system occurs when a class is divided – the boys know what behaviour is expected of them in the other classroom and they realise that they will be rewarded for their behaviour by a different teacher. The quality of the pupil-teacher interaction is very much at the core of this more flexible approach. The increasing use of Circle Time at classroom level helps to address serious pupil issues and increase pupil participation in class decisions.

The Future is Full of Hope

The seeds of the Ballymun Masterplan are coming into bloom with dramatic changes evident in the physical environment of the town. In the Main Street and adjoining housing developments with their unique diversity of shape, scale and design, the extent of the regeneration is a visible reality. Many ask: will bricks and mortar alone change the negative influences within community? At Holy Spirit Boys' School the evidence is that a 'culture of care' assists true regeneration. An improved physical environment is essential, but genuine interest in and concern for young people and their families is what will make new things possible for all. Teachers, at an individual level and as members of a school staff, can make a difference, whatever their source of inspiration.

It may be timely to refer to the old adage 'an ounce of prevention is worth a pound of cure'. A variety of approaches will be necessary. It is the policy of the school, for example, to place a strong emphasis on self-discipline through the provision of different sporting activities: hurling, Gaelic football, soccer and chess. After-school clubs are funded through the local Drugs Task Force targeting those pupils needing extra support. Such pupils are helped with homework and provided with a snack. When their work is complete they are encouraged to use the computers and play games.

For the minority of pupils not fully participating in 'the culture of care', the way forward may be to promote individual behaviour management plans with specific target setting and more effective differentiation in the learning process. A whole-school approach to the deep-seated problem of challenging behaviour is essential if the children, the school and the community are to grow, mature and contribute to the building up of a caring, respectful and generous society which encourages each individual to develop to their fullest potential.

'Any teacher who wants to, can make a difference'
(Anon).

Notes

1. See S. Power, 'The Development of the Ballymun Housing Scheme, Dublin, 1965-1969' *Irish Geography* 33 (2000), pp. 199-212.
2. See S. Power, 'The Development of the Ballymun Housing Scheme', p. 200.
3. See S. Power, 'The Development of the Ballymun Housing Scheme', p. 200.
4. See S. Power, 'The Development of the Ballymun Housing Scheme', p. 201.
5. See *Irish Building and Contract Journal*, July 1964.
6. See National Archives, Box 622, N-228-16.
7. See S. Power, 'The Development of the Ballymun Housing Scheme', p. 209.
8. See S. Power, 'The Development of the Ballymun Housing Scheme', p. 209.
9. See *Evening Herald*, 15 December 1971.
10. See *Irish Press*, 3 July 1969.
11. F. McDonald, *The Construction of Dublin* (Cork: Gandon Editions, 2000), p. 250.
12. See *Ballymun Regeneration News*. Available from www.brl.ie
13. See www.brl.ie
14. See *Ballymun Regeneration Progress Report* (2001-2002), p. 23.
15. Holy Spirit Boys National School, *Daily Report Book*, No. 1.
16. A. Smith, *Discipline for Learning: A Positive Approach to Teaching and Learning Manual*, p. 79, unpublished.
17. See Rogers, B. *Behaviour Management: A Whole-School Approach* (London: Paul Chapman Publishing, 2000), p. 149.
18. See M. Martin, *Discipline in Schools: Report to the Minister for Education, Niamh Bhreathnach*, Spring 1997, pp. 104-109.

TOWARDS INCLUSIVITY IN RELIGIOUS EDUCATION

Martina Ní Cheallaigh

In order to change and to become more open to others, we must first recognise that we need to change.[1]

Life is made up of moments. 'Epiphany' describes those moments when something ordinary and everyday takes on new meaning. In one particular moment of time the way in which we view life can be radically altered. Such moments challenge us to view life differently. They force us to rethink our beliefs and values.

For me, personally, one such 'moment' occurred with the death of my brother. From a sense that I belonged to a community, this tragic event plunged me into an experience of isolation. I no longer belonged. Life was empty. The faith I had been raised in held no answers for me, nor did it offer any comfort. This experience and the ongoing struggle to make sense of my world increased my awareness concerning all those who feel marginalized, by society, by Church, and by many another of life's institutions. It also culminated in a decision on my part to work alongside students with learning disabilities, a group which, in my view, had been sidelined by both society and Church.

This article presents some thoughts on inclusion within Church and explores how this can be accomplished through religious education. True participation can only come about where there is openness of heart. In these days the search for perfection pervades all aspects of life while facile appearance takes on more importance than does real substance. Such an unsatisfactory state of affairs requires of all of us that we stop and think about the values we want to pass on to the next generation. The Church, if it is to have relevance, needs to listen to challenging voices and to embrace change where change is needed.

One Body in Christ: Equality in the Church

The Church has a long history of caring for the needs of people with learning disabilities. Indeed Ireland, like many other countries, has depended on the Church for many years for the provision of schooling and services. Yet it does not seem that this caring service was carried out in a spirit of equality. The focus lay on what could be done for those with learning disabilities, rather than on seeing people with learning disabilities as equals within the Christian community, and who, themselves, have something of value to offer. It is true to say that a lot of excellent work has been done in the past and is still being done today in terms of service provision but one needs to question if, on its own, this is enough. If it is accepted that all are made in the image and likeness of God (Genesis 1:27) then the invitation to belong fully in Christ's Body, the Church, ought to be made to all equally. All should be viewed, not merely as recipients of what the community has to offer, but as participators and contributors who themselves have something of importance and value to offer the community. This inclusion must be genuine. It is not enough merely to make churches physically accessible, although that itself would be an excellent start. Attitudes and prejudices must also be confronted. During a sermon preached while the Special Olympics were taking place in Ireland in the summer of 2003 it was stated that people with learning disabilities were reminders of Christ's crucifixion and of his suffering. Such an attitude, though well-intended no doubt, is far from helpful. What I have learned from people with learning disabilities is the importance of living life in the present, of approaching life with joy, and of forgiving those who have done us wrong. Through my 'teachers' who happen also to be my students, I have become aware of my own prejudices. Jean Vanier and Henri Nouwen both describe the richness brought to their lives through their encounter with people with learning disabilities. Their exclusion, whether conscious or not, denies the Church invaluable opportunities for growth and development.

The culture of consumerism prevalent today presents a materialistic ideal of perfection. Much of society has become caught up in a race towards the 'perfect' body, the 'perfect' job, the 'perfect' life. It is the duty of Christians, to propose and provide other images of what being human is all about. A Christian perspective ought to be accepting of difference and must incorporate a real sense of belonging. The Christian way of life needs to uphold difference, not as something to be tolerated until it can be assimilated into the whole, but as something to be celebrated and embraced as part of the wonder of creation.

Emeritus Professor of Religious Education, John Hull, who is himself blind, makes the point that when Jesus rose from the dead, he was radiant, with his wounds still present.[2] His was not a 'perfect' body, but a body visibly wounded. Nancy Eisland, author of *The Disabled God,* also refers to this woundedness of Christ and its message for Christians when she says:

Jesus, the resurrected Saviour, calls for his frightened companions to recognise in the marks of impairment their own connection with God, their own salvation. In so doing, this disabled God is also the revealer of a new humanity. The disabled God is not only the one from heaven but the revelation of true personhood; underscoring the reality that full personhood is fully compatible with the experience of disability.[3]

What news! Christ, in rising from the dead, rose for all who have been hurt and wounded by life, and for all who have experienced isolation. All are central to Christ's resurrection; all are included at this pivotal moment. This one moment gives Christians their call in life, a call towards greater inclusion, acceptance and empathy for those who have traditionally found themselves on the sidelines but who are now part of the living embodiment of Christ on earth. What better message for Christians to live than the message of the resurrection? Such believers are examples and apostles of brokenness?[4] Instead of seeing people with learning disabilities as symbols of suffering they ought to be embraced as symbols of the resurrection and as a new humanity connected to God through woundedness. Brett Webb-Mitchell, in his book, *Unexpected Guests at God's Banquet,* makes the point that:

> People rarely 'suffer' from having a disability like a sensory impairment, developmental disability, or physical impairment, unless they are physically ill. What they are suffering from is the harshness of the world around them, and the cruelty and oppression in the continual assault found in the great effort to transform everyone who is different to be 'just like me', rather than

more like themselves – the person that God created them to be.[5]

Christians, as followers of Christ, the broken one, need to develop a spirit of openness and welcome for all. The challenge remains to look at each other with God's eyes, and to see in each other the wonderful miracle of creation.

Religious Education: Celebrating the Uniqueness of Those We Teach

Moral theologian Paul Waddell, states that when we come together at worship, it is not the fact that we are able-bodied or disabled that is most important but that we are one in Christ. Acceptance of this oneness in Christ can only lead towards the development of more meaningful, expansive celebrations. He goes on to comment:

> The Church is faithful to the love of God when it realises everyone is indispensable to God, and thus should be indispensable to us. We must train ourselves to behold one another as God does.[6]

All human beings have the right to be told of the love God has for them, both by word and deed. However, those who have been left aside and isolated by society are perhaps more in need of hearing the good news. Wolf Wolfensberger,[7] a leading figure in special education, reminds us that Christians are meant to be a light in the world and that when people with learning disabilities are excluded from religious education or worship we implicitly consent to their overall marginalisation in society. He calls upon all to stand against the marginalisation of people with disabilities reminding us that those physical symbols of inclusion, such as ramps and hearing aid systems, are not enough. A more radical response is needed; one that confronts deeply held attitudes and challenges all to journey and share with people who have learning disabilities.

In approaching the issue of inclusiveness within the Church, it is not enough to deal with physical barriers to inclusion. Attention must also be paid to substance, for instance how religious faith can be celebrated in a way that embodies the gifts of all who attend services and religion classes. Central to this work is the school. Religion is a core subject in the majority of schools and so stands at the centre of any work being undertaken with regard to equality and the Church.

Mary Therese Harrington is a member of the Chicago Archdiocesan Pastoral Team for Special Religious Education (SPRED). In *Developmental Disabilities and Sacramental Access* she lists four main aims of each religion class. These are the development of a sense of the sacred, a sense of the people of God, a sense of Christ and the development of a movement towards God in faith, hope and love.[8] These are general aims, accommodating all students in a religion class. It is important to remember that one's intention should always be to include all, rather than to make one particular group the sole focus of attention. The central aim of any religion class must be to bring all the students into closer relationship with God. How we do this may need to be differentiated for our students but the central aim remains constant.

Developing a religious education class that is differentiated according to students' needs, demands a high level of creativity on the part of teachers, a keen knowledge of the students, and a willingness to break away, where necessary, from the set programme.

The *Alive-O*[9] textbooks in use in Irish primary schools, offer a springboard of rich ideas and teaching methods that the teacher can use to create an individualised curriculum. Such a curriculum will invariably be rich in concrete visual symbol and will focus on colour, art, dance and music rather than merely on language. It is important, in each religion lesson, to move from the human to the holy, beginning each lesson with the student's own experience of life and making the connection with God, and God's place in that person's life. God's presence in everyday life needs to be focused upon if a true relationship with the Creator is to be formed. The idea that God resides in a quiet peaceful church, away from the daily hustle and bustle of human lives is to be avoided. For the connection between life experience and God's presence to be made it is vital that lessons are grounded in the concrete. Only then will the relationship between faith and life be fully understood.

Sharing our Faith is a programme developed by St Joseph's Pastoral Centre, Westminster.[10] Its purpose is to involve people with learning and communication difficulties in the spiritual life of the parish, an aim that it sees as intrinsic to catechesis. The approach used in this programme is one of symbolic catechesis. It is an intuitive approach, grounded in the concrete, while rich in symbol and ritual. It celebrates the strengths of people with learning disabilities. The approach is built on the 'now,' remembering that the present time holds much more interest and relevance to people with learning disabilities than does either the past or the future. The senses act as powerful tools in gathering information from present experience. Nothing should be allowed to distract from their power or take away from the potency of the intuitive response. It is by intuition that one hopes that children and adults with learning difficulties will make the leap from human experience to the mystery of God. This programme is noted as an example of what needs to be borne in mind when preparing religion lessons. Intuition cannot be over-emphasised as a pathway to God. Therefore the senses need to be fully engaged in the work of teaching and learning.

A lively trust in God's ability to bring to completion what we as humans have begun is central to any engagement in religious education. The Holy Spirit is a hidden presence in any religion lesson prompting the individual to action as he or she journeys towards God. No one can really know where another person is in their relationship with God, but one can, however, provide the space to allow this relationship grow and flourish.

Challenges to be addressed
While it is the responsibility of teachers to differentiate the curriculum according to the needs of their particular students, it is important that they do feel supported in their work. In this regard teachers in Special Education must face a number of specific challenges when teaching religion.

- Firstly teachers involved in Special Education have to adapt the curriculum in all subjects to suit the needs of their students. Sufficiency of planning time is therefore, a very real issue for overworked teachers. Guidelines on adaptation of the *Alive-O* programme are needed. A booklet encompassing the material covered in the *Alive-O* series, suggesting ways of approaching each theme and providing age- and need-appropriate resources would be most helpful in assisting teachers in this work in the area of special needs.
- The lack of suitable resources and materials is another important issue. The importance of engaging all of the

student's senses when teaching religion has already been noted. It follows that resources such as clutter-free posters, storyboards and suitable worksheets are needed in addition to simple songs, poems and stories presented in an age- and need-appropriate way.

- In the post-primary section of special schools the *Alive-O* programme may be cognitively suitable, but inappropriate in terms of presentation or ancillary materials. The development of resources appropriate to adolescents is essential. Resources such as photographs of their peer group and materials that reflect their stage in life are vital. In the stories used and themes approached during religion class there must also be recognition of the moral issues faced by these adolescents.

- Finally, the development of parish links remains a difficult task for special schools, particularly where students come from a wide catchment area. Discussion is needed at diocesan and parish level on how these links can best be brought about. Parish groups need to take responsibility in facilitating participation of people with learning disabilities in their parish.[11] Further education and discussion is needed on the part of all those involved in parish work and religious education in order to ensure that the wishes of individuals with learning disabilities are taken into account. It has to be recognised that people with learning disabilities have the same rights as people in the general population and therefore need to be given the choice to accept or refuse a place within the Church community. People with learning disabilities, and others, who are marginalized by society, need to be invited and listened to if genuine inclusiveness is to take place.

Conclusion

All Christians need to be invited to speak, to share their experiences, and to take an active role in their Church. This is crucial if Christians are to become symbols of the resurrection in an increasingly secularised society. The inclusion at the heart of the Church of people with learning disabilities is, in essence, a justice issue. Through the resurrection, woundedness has been transformed and made new. To exclude people on the basis of difference is therefore both unacceptable and foolhardy. Religious educators, particularly, have a duty to promote genuine inclusiveness within schools and to inculcate an attitude based on the acceptance and celebration of difference rather than simply on tolerance alone. As Deborah Creamer, who herself has experienced the reality of disability, says:

If we recognise our connection to our bodies and to each other, we can begin to break down some of the barriers of 'us' and 'them', and begin to build community based on our common (yet different) experiences. In the end, we are all more alike than different, even though we are all different.[12]

Notes

1. J. Vanier, *Our Journey Home: Rediscovering a Common Humanity Beyond Our Differences* (London: Hodder & Stoughton, 1997), p. 205.
2. Reference, John Hull, 'Exploring Spirituality and Disability,' paper delivered at St John of God Conference Centre, Stillorgan, Dublin, 31 January 2004 as recorded and understood by the author of this article who participated in the conference.
3. N. Eisland, *The Disabled God: Towards a Liberatory Theology of Disability* (Nashville: Abingdon Press, 1994), p. 100.
4. See J. Hull reference at note 2 above.
5. B. Webb-Mitchell, *Unexpected Guests at God's Banquet: Welcoming People With Disabilities Into the Church* (New York: Crossroad Publishing, 1994), p. 74.

6. P.J. Wadell, 'Pondering the Anomaly of God's Love: Ethical Reflections on Access to the Sacraments' in E. Foley (ed.) *Developmental Disabilities and Sacramental Access: New Paradigms for Sacramental Encounters* (Collegeville, MN: The Liturgical Press, 1994), p. 70.

7. See W.C. Gaventa, and D.L. Coulter, (eds.) *The Theological Voice of Wolf Wolfensberger* (New York: The Haworth Press, 2001).

8. See M.T. Harrington, 'Affectivity and Symbol in the Process of Catechesis' in E. Foley (ed.) *Developmental Disabilities*, pp. 53-72.

9. See Irish Episcopal Commission on Catechetics, *Alive-O* (Dublin: Veritas, 1996-2004).

10. J. Edwards, *Sharing Our Faith: Involving People with Learning and Communication Difficulties in the Spiritual Life of the Parish Community* (Essex: Matthew James Publishing, 1997).

11. See article by Peg Caverley elsewhere in this collection of essays.

12. See Deborah Creamer, 'Finding God in Our Bodies: Theology From the Perspective of People With Disabilities, Part One', *Journal of Religion in Disability and Rehabilitation* 2/1(1995), pp. 27-42.

WELCOMING THE 'NEW IRISH'

Celebrating Diversity in the Irish Catholic Primary School

Mícheál Kilcrann

'I would like to offer a special word of greeting to the 'new Irish', those who have come to our shores in recent years. My hope is that they will always experience a sense of welcome and of belonging.'[1]

Archbishop Diarmuid Martin, 26 April 2004

A popular song with Irish emigrants over the years includes the line, 'If we only had old Ireland over here'. Nostalgic feelings for the ancestral land would well up in the hearts of the revellers at the singing of these words. However, for those returning to their Irish homeland after the absence of a decade or more, one thing is now glaringly obvious: 'old Ireland' has most definitely given way to 'new Ireland'. The new Ireland in question, however, is one that was hardly envisaged by either long-departed emigrants or green-tinted revolutionaries. The land of the Celtic Tiger is now home to a vast array of peoples of various accents, cultures, religions and skin hues. In short, Ireland is now a multicultural society. This changing scenario, evident throughout the country, presents a challenge to the 'indigenous Irish' – a challenge that is characterised both by promise and by pain. The purpose of this article is to explore the challenge as it pertains to education generally and to religious education particularly. A beginning will be made by reflecting on how Irish society has responded so far to this newfound and growing diversity.

Response of Irish People

The response of Irish people to the multicultural situation has been somewhat mixed. At times it has been positive, at other times negative. One reads approvingly and proudly of the acceptance and welcome accorded to 'the new Irish'[2] by the 'old Irish' whenever positive responses are evident and are reported. However, there are also indications of a disturbingly high number of incidents of antagonism, rejection, insult, prejudice, and injury experienced by some of the immigrants who have come to Ireland. Besides responses that may be classified as either positive or negative there are also those which may be classified as being indifferent. Both negativity and indifference ignore people's real needs, thereby depriving and robbing them of their dignity. What all of this highlights is the urgent need for reflection and planning so that appropriate action may be taken. In this respect education has a key role to play. *The Primary School Curriculum* rightly states:

> The relationship between education and society is dynamic and interactive. Education not only reflects a society but is an influence in shaping its development.[3]

This attitude is reinforced by the teaching profession as is evident from the following remarks of John Carr, the General Secretary of the Irish National Teachers' Organisation (INTO):

> Education holds the key to developing an inclusive society where social diversity and cultural differences can

be respected, promoted and practised ... Schools that reflect and affirm diversity of cultures, ethnicity and religious background will help children from ethnic minorities to feel valued, accepted and supported.[4]

It is therefore to education one must look in seeking a way to create a tolerant, gracious and welcoming approach to growing diversity within communities.

Role of Education

Education informs minds and hearts so as to engender responsible action that is free from prejudice and bias and that exhibits traits of justice and tolerance. Education takes place from the earliest moments of human existence to the drawing of one's last breath. It includes the formation of attitudes and opinions and is heavily influenced by the media – audio, video, print and electronic. In helping to highlight the reality of diversity and multiculturalism in Ireland, various sectors of the media have played an important and responsible role. In general, media voices have avoided the temptation to label and stereotype people and have been, indeed, to the forefront, in advocating a welcoming and tolerant attitude to newcomers to the country and in arguing in favour of legislation which is just, inclusive, and welcoming.

Besides the education which derives from media and cultural sources there is also the more formal education that is transmitted in classrooms and schools around the country. It is in schools that minds are informed, hearts are touched, attitudes developed and practices inculcated. It is encouraging therefore to note the positive attitude to the issue of diversity to be found in education documents that have appeared in recent years. For instance, the Government

White Paper on education, *Charting our Education Future*, heralds the challenge of education in a multicultural society by stating that:

> Recent geopolitical developments, including major changes in Eastern Europe, concern about an apparent resurgence of racism, violence and xenophobia in many countries ... serve to underline the importance of education in areas such as human rights, tolerance, mutual understanding, cultural identity.[5]

The kind of education which best serves this agenda is known as intercultural education. Today, the term 'interculturation' is favoured over that of multiculturalism for the simple reason that the latter may solely be knowledge-based whereas the former implies engagement between the cultures. To all concerned with the development of society, this presents a challenge. Having noted that Ireland already is a multicultural society and that it is moving even more in that direction, attention will now be directed to what is understood by intercultural education.

Intercultural Education
Intercultural education is based on the general aim of enabling individuals develop together along with the society in which they are being raised. Intercultural education is suitable for all children regardless of race or nationality. It comprises two components. One fosters knowledge, understanding, skills and attitudes appropriate for living in a country with a diverse population. The second promotes equality. It challenges discrimination in school and in the education system. Intercultural education is for all pupils.

According to a 1997 EU Socrates/Comenius document, intercultural education has the following objectives:[6]

- To teach children and young people, irrespective of origin or status, how to deal with cultural differences and diversity in society and in their field of personal experience to give them the necessary skills, knowledge and attitudes to acquire the ability
- To promote tolerance, mutual respect and understanding, openness to individuals and groups with a different cultural, ethnic, national or religious background
- To combat racism, xenophobia, discrimination, prejudice and stereotyping
- To provide teachers with additional professional skills so that they can work effectively in classes where young people are from culturally and ethnically mixed backgrounds
- Intercultural education should be integrated throughout the school curriculum. It includes dialogue with the ethos of the school and seeks to become central to all areas of the school plan.

For effective intercultural education to occur, however, it must engage people in the issue at an emotional level, developing thereby a sense of empathy with others. The stance which a teacher ought to have in regard to this issue is clearly spelt out in *The Challenge of Diversity: Education Support for Ethnic Minority Children*. According to this document intercultural education includes three main elements:

(i) Everyone has to be able to understand, speak, read and write the language mainly used in the society . . . This underlines the right of every child to learn the majority language of the society where he/she grows up

(ii) everyone has the right to maintain his/her cultural and linguistic identity. This underlines the right of every child to learn his/her mother tongue

(iii) everyone must learn to respect other cultures and have a basic knowledge about different cultures. It is also important to learn to appreciate the diversities in a multicultural society. This underlines the need for an education about tolerance, human rights and democracy.[7]

It is important, when engaging in intercultural education, to bear in mind that what is being aimed at is not assimilation of the new cultures into the dominant and prevailing one. That would result in a loss of identity on the part of the minority. Rather the goal is integration, not assimilation. Differences are not removed or brushed aside. Rather they are recognised and valued for what they are. Again this point is emphasised by the teaching profession:

> In schools where ethnic minority children are enrolled, intercultural education must aim to ensure the integration of the ethnic minority child into the school while, at the same time, ensuring that this child does not lose his/her ethnic identity and cultural values. In this sense, an opportunity is provided for the education of both the majority and the minority communities in Irish society.[8]

This underlines the need for intercultural education to be addressed to both the majority and the minority communities within schools and classrooms. There ought to be a two-way interaction at play which the teacher needs to be aware of:

> For the majority, it is mainly a matter of learning to live in a multicultural society and to respect and accommodate diversities. For the minority, the central need is to learn the skills and knowledge required to achieve linguistic and cultural identity.[9]

The role of the school in this essential work is clearly set forth in an *Information Leaflet for Parents of Asylum-Seeker and Refugee Children attending Primary Education*. It claims that:

> Irish primary schools promote tolerance, mutual respect and an understanding of cultural, ethical, racial, social and religious diversity. They also promote the reality of difference within an intercultural society. The celebration of intercultural diversity is, for many schools, becoming an important component of school life particularly through their experiences in music, art, dance, history, etc. The school is a multicultural environment. Every child's ethnic origin and religion is respected. It is important that all children will also respect other children in the school.[10]

It is to the practical challenge of educating about and celebrating diversity in the classroom that attention is now turned noting the INTO exhortation that, 'Teachers are encouraged to look at the many opportunities for incorporating intercultural education in the curriculum.'[11]

Promoting Intercultural Education in the School and Classroom

Developing an intercultural ethic in the classroom requires a high level of involvement and dedication. At a practical level there is a great deal that a teacher can do in school and classroom to promote a sense of acceptance and a positive approach to multiculturalism. With imagination and energy a teacher can succeed in putting much in place. Some of the practical means of doing this can include:

Language and Literature

One possible suggestion is to introduce some words or phrases native to non-national children in one's classroom so as to communicate a spirit of belonging and acceptance. One of the easiest and most effective ways to adapt to a multicultural classroom is to use a resource that teachers can sometimes take for granted in their school, namely the library. There are a substantial number of books published for children today that give a clear understanding of mutual respect, values, and rights, as well as an opportunity to feel welcomed, and understood. In the publication *Changing Faces, Changing Places*,[12] for instance, the authors acknowledge diversity as is evident from the sub-title, *A Guide to Multicultural Books for Children*.

Drama

Drama is one of the most important aspects of the young child's development. There is much potential here for multicultural education and it can be great fun at the same time. Through drama children get to try out various roles, as well as practising behaviours, and adopting character changes which differ from what they are used to. In drama no one cultural group should be over represented in the situation.

Music

Today there is a wide variety of music that reflects the culture from which it originates. Ireland is famous for its folk songs many of which have been recorded by popular artists. The same is true of the music of other countries and cultures. This ensures that children have the opportunity to experience music from a variety of cultures.

Physical Education

Children all over the world play similar games but many have different rules and conditions depending on the culture in question. Introducing a variety of games from different cultures requires ingenuity. The sharing of these games within a classroom situation can enable children to have a better understanding of the cultural background and milieu of their new friends.

Beyond these examples there are many other areas of the curriculum, such as geography, history, art and cooking, for instance, that can contribute to the generation of multicultural consciousness on the part of the children potentially leading to mutual acceptance of the richness of diversity.

The Contribution of Religious Education

Religious education has a key role to play in regard to intercultural education. It is important to acknowledge and explore this assertion, especially as religion may be seen by some as a stumbling block to inclusiveness. As a counter to this one needs to recall, first of all, that a key element of intercultural education is the promotion of a positive attitude towards diversity. This point is emphasised by a range of commentators. Former President of Ireland and UN High Commissioner for Refugees, Mary Robinson states that what is required is 'an attitude of mind that we are enriched in Ireland by those who come from other countries.'[13] Former INTO General Secretary, Senator Joe O'Toole, supports this by claiming: 'There is a huge burden of responsibility on us to present this diversity as an adornment and an embellishment of our society.'[14]

The question therefore arises as to just how religion can be a positive element in intercultural education. Religion is about right relationship – right relationship with oneself, with one's fellow humans and with God. Religions subscribe to a belief in God, a God who is Creator. As creator, God is therefore creator of diversity. Diversity, accordingly, ought to be seen and accepted and welcomed, in the religious context, as a gift from God and as a reflection of God in whose image people are created and formed. Diversity, as such, therefore, can be viewed as something of intrinsic value. If, as many believe, the human person is created in the image and likeness of God, then certain aspects of God must be apparent in and through those who are different to oneself – aspects of God to which one otherwise would not have access.

The challenge of diversity may be summarised in terms of 'Three R's': Recognition, Respect, and Response. Religion can contribute in no small way to the promotion of the values associated with these 'Three R's' by enabling its adherents to recognise difference, respect difference, and respond to difference. The biggest obstacle to acceptance of otherness is not religion itself but rather the self-centredness of the human heart. Self-interest feeds off and feeds into prejudice and bias. A religion such as Christianity, for instance, is rooted in the transcendence of the self so as to facilitate a reaching out to God and to other people in the name of and out of love for the Divine. A Francis of Assisi could embrace the otherness of the leper, not out of any human attraction, but out of a love inspired by the love of Christ that Francis accepted and believed in. One might claim the same in respect of Damian of Molokai, Teresa of Calcutta and myriads of others throughout the Christian centuries. Their Christian commitment did not deter them from reaching out. Rather it provided the very motivation and inspiration to so do. This should come as no surprise given the other-orientation which Jesus endeavoured to inculcate in his listeners and followers. Genuine religion teaching therefore, challenges one's attitude and response to people and to situations and issues such as racism and exclusion.

An example of this may be found in the parable of the Good Samaritan. To appreciate the significance of this pivotal Christian story in the present discussion, it is useful to recall that one of the main goals of intercultural education is the combating of racism, a point repeatedly made in the literature on the subject: 'Intercultural education is about respecting cultural difference and promoting anti-racism,'[15] and, 'Intercultural education provides opportunities to create positive responses and strategies to fight racism.'[16] In this parable which Jesus used to illustrate the meaning of neighbour, the stricken man (a Jew) is helped by a member of another race (a Samaritan). Arising from this, the claim can be justified that authentic religious education ought to contribute significantly to genuine reaching out to and acceptance of those who are different to oneself. Keeping these ideas in mind will assist in seeing how the current religion programme in use in Irish Catholic schools, *Alive-O*, can be used to promote the aims and objectives of intercultural education.

The *Alive-O* programme is an all-embracing programme. It is written with a view to welcoming the stranger. It encourages consciousness of those living on the margins of society. It is both child friendly and teacher friendly. The programme is presented and written in accordance with the culture and the changing society in which Irish children are now living. It responds to the nature of the child as one who is full of life, fun, energy and joy

Where the cultural background in the lesson is different, it is relatively easy to replace situations, or contexts to meet the needs of a particular class or group of children. Names can be changed or abbreviated, classroom tasks can be held by either boys or girls, location can be town or country and language can be matched to the children's understanding. A teacher can create an open and caring environment in which to present these situations, where children, irrespective of their own background, can feel valued. This enables them to develop as people and helps them to have respect for themselves, for others and for the world around them.

Primary religious education holds the key to developing an inclusive society where social diversity and cultural difference can be respected, promoted and practised. The importance of such considerations is not just confined to religious educators in the school. Everyone seriously interested in education for the future needs to have an interest in these issues. Schools are important places for the formation of attitudes, and children are influenced by the accepted modes of behaviour and attitude that permeate the school. There is no easy answer to intercultural education. The hard truth is that it involves commitment and requires determination in order to address and cater for the diversity that faces the schools and classrooms of today. In order that all may live together in the same society there is need for a preparedness to look beyond parts of one's own cultural and distant historical past in the interest of promoting a more inclusive and hope-filled future. Education, including religious education, has a key role to play in this endeavour both theoretically and practically. The cost of change will be worth it when set against the promise and possibility of community, of acceptance, of inclusiveness, and of welcome of all, by all, and for the good of all.

Notes

1. Archbishop Diarmuid Martin, 26 April 2004. Available from: www.dublindiocese.ie [Accessed 23 June 2004].
2. See 'The New Irish' a title given to a series of articles on newcomers to Ireland. *The Irish Times Series*, 9-19 May 2004.
3. Department of Education and Science, *The Primary School Curriculum: Introduction* (Dublin: The Stationary Office, 1999), p. 6.
4. Irish National Teachers' Organisation, *Intercultural Guidelines for Schools*, Foreword (Dublin: INTO Publications, 2002).
5. Department of Education, *Charting our Education Future* (Dublin: The Stationary Office, 1995), p. 204.
6. See Department of Education and Science, *Information Booklet on Asylum Seekers, 2001*, p. 12.
7. Irish National Teachers' Organisation, *The Challenge of Diversity: Education Support for Ethnic Minority Children*. (Dublin: INTO Publications, 1998), pp. 35-36.
8. *The Challenge of Diversity*, p. 50.
9. *The Challenge of Diversity*, p. 35.
10. *Information Leaflet for Parents of Asylum Seeker and Refugee Children attending Primary Education*, prepared by the Reception and Integration Agency (August 2001), pp. 5-6
11. *The Challenge of Diversity*, p. 36.
12. S. Coghlan, M. Fitzpatrick and L. O'Dea (eds.) *Changing Faces, Changing Places: A Guide to Multicultural Books for Children* (Dublin: O'Brien Press, 2001).
13. See Mary Robinson, *The Irish Times* (9 March 1998) reporting on a major forum on human rights held in Dublin, March 1998.
14. *The Challenge of Diversity*, Joe O'Toole, p. ii.
15. *Intercultural Guidelines for Schools*, Card 1, Introduction.
16. *Cultural Diversity*, p. 50

THE WISDOM OF FRIEDRICH FROEBEL AND ST BENEDICT

A *Support for Teachers of Distressed Children Today*

Carmel Scanlon

Why, oh why did I choose this career? I'm only two years teaching and I'm so disillusioned. It is nothing like I imagined it would be. So many of the children are disturbed, antisocial and disinterested. Marriages seem to be breaking down all over the place. All the solid values are gone. There seems to be no accountability and we as teachers are expected to pick up all the pieces. If only this group of children were not in the class I'd be fine. They keep acting up, looking for negative attention and disrupting others. It is not teaching, it is policing. I feel like I am doing time.

These are real comments from a real teacher suffering from strain, stress, exhaustion and disappointment. What she describes is not an isolated incident. In the cultural mayhem of disintegrating family, community and spiritual structures, common in Ireland today, children are suffering starkly, undeservedly, heartbreakingly and teachers are suffering with them. Is it naïve to believe anything can help in this situation? Is there any realistic way that teachers can encourage, guide and help these children while at the same time finding satisfaction and fulfilment in teaching as a profession?

Drawing on the wisdom and insights of St Benedict the founder of monasticism, and Friedrich Froebel the great German educator, this article contends that teachers can enjoy rather than endure their work with distressed children in their care.

Benedict offers educators a grounded spirituality and way of life that facilitates stability, balance, community and meaning for teachers today, a spirituality that has stood the test of time over one and a half thousand years, a spirituality that is suitable for the ordinary person in everyday circumstances. His Rule has been described as 'simply a piece of Wisdom literature designed to deal with the great questions of life in ways that make them understandable, clear and achievable'[2]

Froebel, on the other hand, offers awareness, understanding and profound insight into the suffering behind the behaviour of these children so that rather than being threatened by their antisocial acting out in the classroom, teachers are confident and at ease when handling their difficulties and distress.

Equipped with Froebel's insights and imbued with this Benedictine spirit, the teacher begins to mirror the loving kindness of Jesus Christ. This spirit permeates the classroom. These children can then experience love, affirmation, acceptance and safety – perhaps for the first time.

Acknowledging Where Children are Coming From

Children do not arrive in the classroom untouched by their social background and environment. Their home situation leaves deep and lasting influences which carry implications for their school lives. An awareness of this fact by the teacher is the first step in facilitating their education and growth.

It was the conviction of Froebel that 'life in all its aspects is connected to make one, harmonious whole' and that, 'There existed 'inter-connectedness' between all things, between our ancestors; the present generation and future generations; between the present life and the life to come.'[3] To Froebel, this meant that, 'there is a link between the education of children in the home, the school and the wider world.[4] Indeed, he went further, insisting that:

> life itself was the most important school for man, and that unless a school was related to life, it had no claim to its name. Living and schooling in that sense were synonymous.[5]

With a policy of open interaction between home and school, educators quickly become aware of the lack of support in the lives of distressed children. Teachers can ponder the family-life of these children which can often be chaotic, unpredictable, stressful, unreliable and uncertain. Teachers, by meeting and involving parents where possible in the school context with a supportive and accepting attitude, rather than a critical one, can create a very important positive, trusting link between the two worlds of the child. This is particularly relevant when home life is difficult, challenging and dysfunctional. Visiting parents in their homes, where possible, especially when the child is in severe distress, can create a bond of trust and support for the parent. That someone cares during a period of crisis or upheaval can help make their difficulties more bearable. Teaching is, after all, a vocation not an occupation. Accordingly, we begin then to appreciate what kind of world some children come from:

- A world where organised religion as a moral guide and a stabilising influence is rarely a significant part of their lives. Very often these children live in a spiritual vacuum in which an explicit relationship with a living, personal God is neither nurtured nor recognised.

- A world where they occupy themselves after school in 'free range' fashion until their parents return from work – or in some cases, sadly, from the local pub – too tired to listen, too drained to hear, and sometimes too emotionally needy themselves to be able or willing to attend to their children. They thus perpetuate, what John Bradshaw calls, 'the crisis of adult children raising children who will become adult children themselves.'[6]
- A world where their bodies are malnourished and hyped-up by living on takeaways, pizzas, crisps, cakes or chocolate bars instead of on a balanced, healthy diet.
- A world where adults often discharge feelings in an unrestrained and erratic manner, which can be distressful and disturbing to the children in their care.
- A world where being treated by adults with respect, dignity and selfless devotion is often foreign to their experience.
- A world where the need for conversation, story, play and adult involvement is replaced by hours of unsupervised TV viewing, indiscriminate video-watching and internet browsing, leaving them vulnerable to exploitation and violence, while pounding them with images of infidelity, deceit and negativity.
- A world where parenting is haphazard at best, discipline is spasmodic, unpredictable and inconsistent, alternating between indulgence and neglect and where the children are bribed with money to do ordinary household chores, while at the same time their basic need for order, routine and predictability are utterly neglected.
- A world where one or both parents may have married out of a need for parenting and nurturing themselves, a situation in

which the mother often becomes overwhelmed and distressed, the father finds someone else, and no one is there emotionally for the children.

• A world where the stability of the family as a coherent reliable group is often non-existent.

Hyped-up on junk food, exhausted from inadequate sleep, physically unfit from endless TV watching instead of engaging in active and wholesome play, they become angry, wild, unmotivated, uncared-for and uncaring.

Having a clear awareness of this situation, the teacher may find it easier to be understanding of the children's failings and their challenging 'bold' behaviour. They are more likely, therefore, to treat them with support and guidance rather than criticism and harshness, bearing in mind the fact that 'a child regards his own family life objectively and takes it as an ideal of life.'[7] There is no point in giving negative feedback to these children because they will only react defensively.

The task of educators, therefore, is to create a safe environment in which guidance and support, along with loving kindness, will enable them to see and experience another way of relating so that they will learn to live, as Froebel says, 'in harmony with themselves, in harmony with their neighbours and the environment, and in harmony with their Creator.'[8]

How These Children Present in Class
These children generally present in class in either of two ways but may show some characteristics of both.

They may withdraw into themselves and all their distress is imploded. This defence is generally adopted by girls though not exclusively so. In this scenario, children become dreamy, distracted, tired, listless and drained. They may complain of physical sickness and pain. In the long term this way of handling their distress can have severe repercussions on their health. 'Emotional energy that is acted in can cause physical problems including gastro-intestinal disorders, headaches, back-aches, neck-aches and severe muscle tension.'[9] By 'acted in', John Bradshaw here means the internalising of negative feelings that are too overwhelming to acknowledge.

Secondly, children may also work extremely hard to 'do well', 'be good', 'be perfect' and 'be in control'. Their thinking often goes as follows: 'If I could control everything no one can catch me off guard and hurt me.'[10] They may, too, shrink from all conflict, argument, honest emotional discussion or engagement with other children because they feel that this would be too threatening to their security. Their relationship with other children therefore, becomes stylised and 'sage' rather than spontaneous and 'real'. Their self-esteem also plummets because they think they are to blame for the problems at home. At first sight this seems irrational, but Alice Miller, the world-renowned Jungian psychoanalyst, in her years of therapeutic work, has discovered that 'children tend to blame themselves for their parents' cruelty and to absolve the parents, whom they invariably love, of all responsibility.'[11] Feeling helpless or abandoned is harder to face than carrying the enormous burden of guilt themselves. 'This toxic guilt is a way of having power in a powerless situation. It tells you that you are responsible for other people's feelings and behaviour.'[12] This can set them up for a co-dependent way of relating as adults later in life. Children who react like this often try to placate authority. They do this because their inner world is so fragile and their sense of self so weakened that any criticism would send them into a distraught spiral of distress. Having rejected themselves, their fear of risking further rejection is unbearable.

Sometimes they are suffused with grief and loss if one parent leaves the home for good. They become 'clingy' in their need for the teacher's approval, trying to glean any care, love, kindness or understanding to help them to keep going. They may show the teacher a letter they have written to the missing parent believing that, if they write of their loss and love, the beloved parent will return. Their abject misery and stunned dismay when they discover the futility of their effort is followed by feelings of worthlessness, shame and despair.

One little boy in the class who had waited at the front window of his home for days, watching for his father's return, reported every day of his optimism about this happening very soon. When he realised eventually that this was never going to occur, he said: 'I mustn't have written the letter properly. Otherwise he'd have come back.'

In sum, these children suffer acutely, endlessly, relentlessly for sins that were not theirs in the first place.

Responding to the Needs of Such Children

Not many years ago the solution to any classroom disturbance would have been to slap the children for their bad behaviour so as to have them 'licked into shape' and forced to conform accordingly. This approach only succeeded in sending the problem underground while relieving the teacher of having to deal in an ongoing way with unruly behaviour.

Nowadays, because of a more holistic approach, the challenge to teachers is greatly increased. How can they make the classroom a safe, supportive place for these children? Arising out of the experience and reflection of this writer, a Froebel-trained teacher, the conviction emerged that fundamental to helping them is an understanding of their key emotional requirements at school, namely respect, acceptance, inclusion, awareness and strength. In considering how to address these needs the work of Froebel has some wisdom to offer.

Respect

The first requirement of these children is a sense of being respected as people in their own right. Froebel believed that his educational ideas 'grew out of the universal truth that a child is an essential member of humanity and as such needs the adults' respect, attention and care.'[13] Indeed, from accounts of his own teaching career we can imagine how he would treat with wholesome dignity a suffering child. An inspector who called to assess Froebel's school in Keilhau, Germany, having heard rumours that it was undisciplined, wrote the following inspiring report at the end of his inspection.

> I found here, what is never and nowhere shown in practical life, a truly and closely united family of some sixty members, living in quiet harmony, all showing that they gladly perform the duties of their various positions.

> A family which is held together because of its strong bonds of mutual confidence and because every member sees the good of the whole, everything – as of itself – thrives in happiness and love.

> With great respect and hearty affection all turn to the Principal. The little five-year old children cling to his knees, while his friends and colleagues hear and honour his advice, with the confidence which his insight and experience and his indefatigable zeal for the good of the whole, deserve.

> While he has bound himself in brotherliness and friendship to his fellow-workers as the support of his life's work, which to him is truly holy work, that this union – this brotherhood – so to speak, among the teachers must have the most salutary influence on the instruction and training and on the pupils themselves is self-evident. The love and respect in which the pupils hold all their teachers find expression in an attention, and an obedience, which render unnecessary almost all disciplinary severity. (Hanschmann 1875:136)[14]

This account of Froebel's school shows that, if the child is respected, everybody gains – including the teacher. Joachim Liebschner, an authority on the work of Froebel, goes on to say that, for Froebel, the children were treated with the same courtesy as everybody else in the community. He also remarks that in all of Froebel's writings, there is not one article on punishment. Modern educational psychology supports Froebel in this regard. For example, child-specialist, Jan Hunt points to the futility of negative correction when she says:

> Punishment teaches a child nothing about how to handle similar situations in the future. Loving support is the only way to learn true moral behaviour based on strong inner values rather than superficially 'good' behaviour based only on fear.[15]

This respect goes even deeper. There is no room for idle, vacuous gossip in the staff room at the expense of these children. It is only too easy to become patronising, righteous and judgemental. Teachers would be well advised to ponder the words of Bradshaw – a leading authority in the field of recovery, dysfunctional families, and inner child work – 'Neither cocaine nor heroin nor any other drug can touch the adrenaline rush of righteousness.'[16]

Acceptance

To feel safe, children need to feel accepted as they are. They need to know that in the classroom everybody belongs and that there are no outsiders. To quote Froebel once more: 'Possessing an immortal soul, [the child] should be cared for as a manifestation of … God's presence, love and grace, as a gift of God.'[17] This acceptance can be reinforced when the child's behaviour needs to be challenged. He can say to himself, for example, 'She likes me but she does not like what I am doing.' In this way, correction does not lower the children's self-esteem, but supports them in developing good behavioural patterns.

Liebschner gives us a very moving account of an event that happened the Sunday before Froebel died in 1852:

> On the Sunday before Froebel's death, one of the children brought some flowers. Froebel greeted the small messenger with great joy. And though he already found it difficult to lift his hand, he held the child's hand and put it to his lips. Froebel now asked us to 'look after the flowers and spare my weeds. I have learned much from both of them.'

> Flowers and weeds, when carefully observed, provided equally important information and were, therefore of equal importance to Froebel, just as intelligent and slow-learning children, conformist and non-conformist children demanded respect. Froebel's belief that beneath every human fault lies a crushed human virtue led him to

> accept even the least intelligent and most difficult children as essential and important members of the community.[18]

This illustrates Froebel's utter acceptance of each child. It is little wonder that they felt so happy and secure in his presence. A task of educators is to bring to light the crushed human virtues, referred to by Froebel. This task will include, particularly in relation to these children who are the subject of this article, a sacred respect for their privacy and personal defences in dealing with their suffering. Any prying, intrusion or interrogation would create major obstacles in trying to make authentic connection with them possible. They are invited to be open and are offered support. However, if they choose not to accept what is on offer, this is respected also. In a paradoxical way, this very sensitivity often results in greater openness. Trust cannot be purchased by coercion nor confidentiality by intrusion.

Inclusion
When the children are involved in the process of making classroom rules they feel in a very real way that it is *their* class, *their* community. In Froebel's schools children were 'encouraged to work together, to help each other and to devise strategies for solving problems corporately.'[19] Asking children to spend their childhood years being good by blindly doing what they are told, and then expecting them to make responsible adult decisions later in life, is setting them up for failure. Learning from an early age to take responsibility and make decisions prepares children to become well-adjusted adults.

When pupils see their class as a community and these rules as a protection of their safety and well-being rather than as imposed from above, they are far more likely to be co-operative and at peace. 'Consensual decision-making in which all can win and none need lose'[20] is more likely to lead to the desirable outcome.

In the homes of many of these children there is commonly a disorder of power in the family dynamic. The relationships are often based on domination and submission rather than on intimacy and respect. Such children need to experience a classroom where each pupil is a valued member and 'each child has a particular gift which will become visible if circumstances are right and freedom for expression of the same is given.'[21] In this way the children experience being respected and are more likely to respect others as a consequence. For example, one little girl who felt she did not have anything to offer the class, on being encouraged by the teacher to be part of the group, responded in surprise, 'You think *I* exist.'

Froebelian schools were run on these principles of mutual support and acceptance. In this environment of co-operation 'children learned to help and respect each other. In Froebel's kindergartens, children grew into well-balanced people and parents noticed changes in their improved behaviour especially towards other children.'[22] They had experienced first-hand co-operation and inclusion rather than competition.

Awareness

'We teach who we are'[23] is an axiom which educators are wise to bear in mind. Teachers with an awareness of their own feelings are far less likely to transfer their 'disowned shadow' to their students. Such teachers are open to the possibility that when a clash occurs between themselves and a particular child the source of the dissonance may be within the teacher and not necessarily something which is caused by the child.

It is also important to have a certain sensitivity in the classroom so as to actively include children who set themselves up for rejection with antisocial behaviour. Educators need to be aware that a child who behaves in a taciturn manner may not, in fact, intend to be offensive. They may have good reason, as Quaker educator Parker Palmer claims, to fear those in power. Experience has taught them that there is safety in not speaking in an 'adult world where they feel alien and disempowered.'[24] He goes on to say that, 'Students' signals are usually signals of fear, not disdain.'[25]

Teachers also need to be aware of the suffering behind the children's behaviour. When they respond in this way with strength and kindness the children feel accepted. Much of the disruptive behaviour often diminishes as a result. Reading the non-verbal signals of these distressed children correctly, therefore, is essential. To enable teachers to so respond it is imperative that they get in touch with their own inner self for as Alice Miller says, 'Our capacity to understand the language of mimicry, of gestures, of behaviour depends on the degree to which we can hear the child within us.'[26]

Strength

These children need to feel that teachers are strong enough to contain their tumultuous feelings without reacting negatively. At the same time, the teacher needs to be gentle, to be kind and sensitive to them as people, to be affirming yet real, acknowledging their own mistakes while being forgiving of the children's. Educators, using moral authority rather than aggressive domination, need to love their students while allowing them to be themselves. To quote Palmer again: 'The highest form of love is a love that allows for intimacy without the annihilation of difference.'[27] This calls for honesty, clarity and integrity so that the children feel utterly secure.

Teachers are there to direct, guide and facilitate the children's education, not to win their approval. They are not the children's therapists, parents or social workers, even though, at times, they may find themselves called upon to exercise some of these roles. There is no room when dealing with these distressed children for indulgent sentimentality. The last thing they need is another weak adult with unclear vacillating values. They require of their teachers strength of character, leadership and loving kindness. As one very challenging boy put it: 'I love being in this class. At last I have found someone who is able for me.' For disruptive children to be disliked, criticised, rejected and labelled is a very lonely place. They need, metaphorically speaking, to be 'lovingly held in a safe place' where classroom boundaries are clear, predictable, and consistent.

Profile of a 'Benedictine' Teacher

A high ideal of the role of the teacher has been advocated above. Having the insights of Froebel alone might not be sufficient to attain this ideal. Teachers can only acquire this depth, strength and wisdom through possession of a solidly grounded spirituality. One example, already mentioned, which has stood the test of time within the Christian tradition, is the Benedictine Way. Conceived in the sixth century by St Benedict and refined over the centuries by his many followers, this Rule or way of life consists of nine key themes. These themes are listening, moderation, balance, authority, prayer, community, work and leisure, stability and sacredness of the ordinary. They can be of great relevance to teachers. While it is not possible to explore in detail these nine themes here it may be useful to ponder how they manifest themselves in the profile of insightfully aware teachers motivated and nourished by Benedict's spirit.

'Benedictine' teachers are educators who, with regular meditation and prayer, have become more and more centred and grounded in Christ, especially, like Benedict, through the Blessed Eucharist which is the source and summit of their lives. From this secure footing they are enabled to live a balanced life of moderation and regularity – allowing time for leisure, work, friendships, study and rest. They have the tenacity to see a job or commitment through to its conclusion and are not afraid to speak out in courage when necessary. Not being one of the 'lemmings of life'[28] they cannot be bought by any system, image, promotion or accolade. They seek only to promote the image of Jesus Christ as they dedicate themselves to the wellbeing of their students.

Imbued, like Froebel, with an attitude of warmth towards children, there is a buzz of shared learning, an atmosphere of kindness, peace and empathy in their classroom. Discipline problems are minimised because the children feel accepted and safe. They know that the teacher is in control and is not spending time fighting to gain and maintain order. Having been taught to be aware of their responsibilities as well as their rights, the children now have time for fun, humour and banter with their teacher. For these children, education becomes a loving experience and 'it is only in this love that they at last become real.'[29]

Through working on their own integrative processes, these teachers are deepening their knowledge of who they are and so have no need to control other people's lives in order to avoid facing their own shadow, i.e. 'the discarded, devalued and 'unacceptable' aspects of soul and self'[30] which need to be befriended and brought into God's light. Indeed, their authority comes from within, from an inner integrity and honesty which uses leadership and strength to serve rather than oppress, to facilitate rather than manipulate. This moral authority is reached through ongoing submission to the action of the Holy Spirit in their lives.

Through living out the Rule of Benedict they can listen in the silence both to what others may never be able to articulate and to their inner selves without censoring or criticising. This very acceptance leads them to have a major moral impact on those they encounter and those they serve. They see that Jesus is to be found in the ordinary, everyday, humdrum details of life. They develop an acceptance of their humanity. As a result their spirituality is humane, grounded, real, and relevant.

Because these teachers dedicate their day to God, they recognise it as grace-filled and they themselves have something to offer the children they teach. They are not often fazed by setbacks or disappointments in the classroom because they know there is only one Saviour; and it is not they. They allow Providence to work through them and leave the results to God. They have cured themselves of 'the affliction of caring how they appear before others. They concern themselves only with how they appear before God.'[31]

Achieving connection and success with distressed children, as many teachers have found, is not an unrealistic pipe dream. This approach has proved over time that it can succeed. It does, however, require very hard work, patience, endurance and committed dedication. It can be very emotionally demanding but is also most rewarding. The alternative to expending oneself on behalf of these children is to allow them to slip through the system and become a burden to themselves and to society in the future.

The Benedictine Way and the insights and wisdom of Froebel help educators to rediscover the energising exhilaration of teaching, the joy of learning, the magic of discovery and the sense of connectedness with children as individuals. By bringing them the love of Jesus Christ, the warmth of acceptance and the safety of a teacher's strength, little faces that were stony and frozen begin to open up and radiate trust. For teachers, it is now no longer just a job, nor an endurance. They discover their true vocation at last and, inspired by Benedict, 'find again the meaning of existence,'[32] 'in this truly holy work.'[33]

Notes

1. F. Froebel (1782-1852), the great German educator, who was responsible for many of the monumental changes which have taken place in the treatment of children.
2. J. Chittister, *Wisdom Distilled from the Daily* (San Francisco: Harper & Row, 1991), p. 8.
3. J. Liebschner, *A Child's Work: Freedom and Play in Froebel's Educational Theory and Practice* (Cambridge: Lutterworth Press, 2001), p. xii.
4. J. Liebschner, *A Child's Work*, p. xii.
5. J. Liebschner, *A Child's Work*, p. 11.
6. J. Bradshaw, *The Family: A New Way of Creating Solid Self-Esteem*, (Deerfield Beach, Florida: Health Communications, 1996), p. 4.
7. I. Lilley, *Friedrich Froebel: A Selection from His Writings* (Cambridge University Press, 1967), p. 123.
8. J. Liebschner, *Foundations of Progressive Education: The History of the National Froebel Society* (Cambridge: Lutterworth Press, 1991), p. 19.
9. J. Bradshaw, *Homecoming: Reclaiming and Championing your Inner Child*, p. 15.
10. J. Bradshaw, *Homecoming*, p. 12.
11. A. Miller, *Pictures of a Childhood* (London: Virago, 1995), p. 177. Alice Miller is a world-famous Swiss psychologist who has made an enormous contribution to our understanding of children's suffering and its consequences. Her books have been translated into twenty-one languages.
12. J. Bradshaw, *Homecoming*, p. 130.
13. J. Liebschner, *Foundations of Progressive Education*, p. 8.

14. J. Liebschner, *Foundations of Progressive Education*, p. 8.
15. J. Hunt, 'Ten Reasons Not to Hit Your Kids', Appendix, A. Miller, *Breaking Down the Walls of Silence to Join the Waiting Child* (London: Virago, 1992), p. 171.
16. J. Bradshaw, *Creating Love* (London: Piatcus, 1992), p. 235.
17. I. Lilley, *Friedrich Froebel: A Selection from His Writings*, p. 57.
18. J. Liebschner, *Foundations of Progressive Education*, p. 7.
19. J. Liebschner *Foundations of Progressive Education*, p. 1.
20. P. Palmer, *The Courage to Teach* (San Francisco: Jossey-Bass, 1998), p. 38.
21. J. Liebschner, *A Child's Work*, p. 36.
22. J. Liebschner, *Foundations of Progressive Education*, p. 17.
23. P. Palmer, *The Courage to Teach*, p. 2.
24. P. Palmer, *The Courage to Teach*, p. 45.
25. P. Palmer, *The Courage to Teach*, p. 48.
26. A. Miller, *Pictures of a Childhood*, p. 24.
27. P. Palmer, *The Courage to Teach*, p. 55.
28. J. Chittister, *Wisdom Distilled from the Daily*, p. 101.
29. T. Merton, *Seeds of Contemplation* (New York: New Directions, 1972), p. 68.
30. C. Pinkola Estes, *Women Who Run with the Wolves* (London: Random House, 1993), p. 236.
31. W.J. Bausch, *The Yellow Brick Road* (Mystic, Connecticut: Twenty-third Publications, 1999), p. 120.
32. Pope John Paul II, Homily at Norcia, 23 March, 1980. Available at http://www.vatican.va/holy_father/john_paul_ii/speeches/1980/march/
33. J. Liebschner, *Foundations of Progressive Education*, p. 8.

APPROACHES TO PRIMARY RELIGIOUS EDUCATION TODAY

ALIVE-O

The Irish Church's Response to the Religious Education Needs of Children

Brendan O'Reilly

The *Children of God* Series, first introduced to Irish Catholic primary schools in 1973, was a new and exciting concept in religious education for primary schools. The programme was received enthusiastically, not only in Ireland, but also in many schools outside the country, particularly in Britain. The importance of keeping in touch with changes and developments in the field of religious education, as well as with the ever-changing face of society, was recognised as an important factor and, so, the first re-presentation of the programme was introduced to schools in 1983. This reflected the insight of *Catechesi Tradendae*, which stated that, 'Catechesis needs to be continually renewed by a certain broadening of its concept, by the revision of its methods, by the search for suitable language, and by the utilisation of new means of transmitting the message.'[1]

Following the publication of the *Catechism of the Catholic Church* in 1992[2] and preceding the publication of the *General Directory for Catechesis* in 1997,[3] the Irish Episcopal Commission on Catechetics deemed it timely to re-present the *Children of God* series for the second time. The first kit in this second re-presentation of the series was made available in 1996. This series is called *Alive-O* and, having been progressively published on an annual basis since 1996, was completed in the summer of 2004.⁴ It is approved by the Irish Catholic Bishops' Conference as the national programme for primary religious education in Ireland and it is also used in Scotland.

The Task of Religious Education

The task of religious education at primary level is to enable children to grow as people of faith. A religious education programme is a resource for teachers, parents, priests and other parish personnel. Of its nature a religious education programme takes on a task that is very different from that of any other programme used in the primary school context. It seeks to help children to be five, seven, ten or twelve-year-olds who are people of faith and who will one day be adults of mature faith. We ask ourselves, what is a person of mature faith? Obviously it is not simply someone who knows certain things, though, of course knowing has its place. It is important that people be as articulate in the area of their religious faith as they are in any other area of their lives – that they can give an account of the faith that is theirs. Faith influences the way in which people understand themselves and their relationships with others, with the natural world and with God.

However, knowing all the right answers does not, of itself, make one a person of faith. Faith involves doing and being as well as knowing. It influences how people make decisions, what they see as being more or less important, how they react to the people and events around them, their hopes for themselves, for what they want to become, and for their world. The *Alive-O* programme approaches growth in faith in such an all-embracing manner. The kind of 'knowing' that the *Alive-O* programme seeks is not only one which leads to clarity of thought and articulation, but one which profoundly influences the whole of an individual's approach to life. It seeks to lead the children to become the kind of people who see the world around them and all that is happening in it through the eyes of faith, and whose interpretations of what is happening and responses to it are all influenced by their faith. The programme seeks to lead children to respond to God here and now with faith, love and gratitude. Therefore, it endeavours to communicate the Christian message to children in a manner appropriate to their age, stage of faith development and life experience.

The Title

The title of the *Alive-O* series is drawn from a saying of Saint Irenaeus of Lyons – '*Gloria Dei vivens homo*'. This quotation is inclusively translated in every teacher's book of the series as: 'The glory of God is people fully alive'. The gospel connection here is unmistakable. Jesus' words, 'I have come that you may have life and have it to the full' (John 10:10), point to a possibility for dialogue between the central core of the gospel and a central concern of the culture. The primary school classrooms of Ireland represent a space where there is a daily encounter between the popular culture and the teaching of the gospel. Having researched the first four available programmes in the *Alive-O* series, Martin Kennedy was able to state that 'Despite the changing environment and the growing gap generally between Church and popular culture, the students' experience of Church and gospel in the classroom is one that they find attractive and engaging.'[5]

A Work of Partnership

The religious education of primary school children is a work of partnership between the home, the school and the parish.

Unlike the past, teachers say that at present many children come to school without having any sense of God and without knowing even the simplest prayers. While there may not always be the level of faith commitment at home that one would wish, there are many parents who are interested in their children's growth in faith, and who sometimes are at a loss as to how they can tune into what is going on in the classroom. In the *Alive-O* programme a number of strategies to help parents to become more involved in their children's religious education are included. There are newsletters provided in the kit which can be sent home a number of times each year; these help parents to be aware of what their children are doing in school and of how it is relevant in terms of what the programme is trying to achieve in religious education. Parents are also invited, when it is possible in the local context, to join in prayer services in the classroom on a number of occasions during the school year. The local priest or other appropriate parish personnel can also be invited to take part in these prayer services. More than any 'talk' these give parents an insight into the spirit of the programme in action and a sense of how they could pray with their own child at home. They also have the potential to bring together all the people from home, from school and from the parish who support and encourage the child' s growth in faith.

The teacher is one of the most significant people in the life of any schoolchild. While the teacher cannot and should not be expected to take on the role of the parent or guardian or make up for what can sometimes be missing from the parent-child relationship, many people will look back on their relationship with a particular teacher as being one of the most formative influences in their lives. A teacher can create in the classroom an open, respectful, caring, trust-filled atmosphere where children can feel valued and have a sense that their uniqueness and potential are recognised. In such an atmosphere they can be helped to develop as people who will have a respect for themselves, for others, for the world in which they live and for God. For many children the school may be the first place where they will feel cared for and valued. While no school can make up for what is missing at home, whatever a teacher can do to give children a sense of being lovable and loved is significant. In the religious education class, a teacher who respects each child and each child's experience, who tries to take where the children are at as a starting-point, can do much to help the children to grow as people of faith.

A teacher can help the children to understand that they are individually known and loved by God, and that God, who has given us the gift of life, is caring for and sustaining that life. She can help the children to become aware of the fact that God is always listening to them and that they can talk to God about their good and their bad experiences. Helping the children to take part in the prayer time during each lesson will lead them to become comfortable with a number of different ways of praying. By encouraging them to be aware of the needs of the others in the class, to share and to be truthful, to care for the environment both inside and outside of the classroom, the teacher can help the children to become people who will have a sense of their inter-dependence on one another, on the physical world and on God. By reminding them to acknowledge, respond to and give thanks for the love and care they receive from those with whom they live at home, the teacher encourages them to see their own potential for being loving caring people. More important than any of this is the example children see in the way in which the teacher responds to each member of the class and the effort made by her or him to create an atmosphere of respect and care among the children for each other.

While a religious education programme, therefore, is a useful resource in the task of communicating faith, it is the individual teacher in each particular classroom who brings the programme, and the faith it seeks to communicate, to life. The *Alive-O* programme offers resources and methodology, but these need to be taken hold of by the teacher, who will be aware of the nuances of his or her particular situation and will communicate the content in a way that is most appropriate to that reality.

The programme also seeks to reach out to the wider parish community. It does so by providing 'Liturgical Links' in order to assist the celebrant of the Sunday Eucharist to make connections with the programmes that the children are following in school. These liturgical ideas are optional and are simply suggestions or pointers. Parishes differ enormously in size, in personnel and in organisational structure. Also there is a great number and variety of primary schools, across the rural/urban divide. Therefore, any suggestion offered by the *Alive-O* programme clearly needs to be adapted to each individual parish context. However, where it is possible to make links, it can only be both affirmative and supportive of what is happening at school, especially when that work is seen to be echoed in the parish liturgies.

The *Alive-O* Programme

Now complete, the programme consists of eight separate kits – one corresponding to each of the eight classes/standards in the primary schools of the Republic of Ireland. It is the responsibility of the Board of Management of every Catholic primary school in the Republic to supply an *Alive-O* kit to every class teacher. The class kit contains a variety of catechetical materials, which hopefully will be of assistance to the class teacher in communicating faith to the children. Among the usual items to be found in the *Alive-O* kit are: the teacher's book, the pupil text, the relevant video tape, music CDs or cassette tapes, a workbook, parent information sheets, liturgical information sheets and other specific materials. Ancillary materials such as A1 size posters for each class, aids on teaching *Alive-O* in multi-class situations, an *Alive-O* handbook for classroom visitations, an overview of the programme, a musical accompaniment for *Alive-O* music, parish resources for confirmation, extra videos, readers and so on are also available.

An Irish language edition of the programme, called *Beo go Deo*, is also available, as is a Scottish edition. By kind permission of the Irish Episcopal Commission on Catechetics, The Church of Ireland Board of Education has developed the *Follow Me* series (based on *Alive-O*), together with the Methodist and Presbyterian Boards of Education. The words of the *General Directory for Catechesis* spring to mind in this context: 'catechesis, therefore, is always called to assume an ecumenical dimension everywhere.'[6]

The Approach

The *Alive-O* programme does not espouse any particular catechetical methodology. The programme uses an eclectic approach, choosing what appears to be the best from diverse sources, media or styles. The junior end of the programme, *Alive-O 1 – Alive-O 4*, follows a process described in the teacher's book as that of *Focus*, *Explore* and *Response*. Here each lesson begins by focusing on particular significant experiences, which are part of the life of a child of that age. Children's experience, particularly in the younger classes, is limited, as is their understanding and vocabulary. It is not easy for an adult to enter into the world of the child and to explore with the child his or her experience, not from the adult's but from the child's point of view. The programme in its choice of experiences seeks to provide the teacher with the resources to do this. Lessons usually begin by offering the children a number of activities, which focus on the particular experience that is being explored in a particular lesson. It may be a game, or a story, or an art activity. The teacher seeks to enable the children to become the kind of people who have eyes that see and ears that hear, people who are capable of a level of awareness that seeks not only to answer the question 'what is this?' but also the question 'what does this mean for me; for me in relation to others? or for me in relation to God?' In this religious education programme the teacher provides the opportunity for the children to stop and think; to ask questions; to explore; to wonder; to come to faith.

Having focused on a particular experience, the children are then offered the possibility of dwelling on the experience that is being explored, so that they may become more aware of what is happening. They may engage in activities such as listening to a story, drawing pictures, acting out a scene, or engaging in a craft activity. It is hoped that they will become more aware of the feelings associated with starting school and be helped to cope with these feelings; or that they will be more alert to the beauty of the world and experience something of the wonder and mystery of the natural world; or that they will have a greater consciousness of the gift of life in their own bodies and feel the excitement of being alive; or that they will be more aware of the creativity of which they are capable and see this as a gift. The *Alive-O* programme explores the Christian story as it sheds light on their experience. It seeks to provide opportunities for the children to become reflective people who will take time to stop and think, so that they will have the capacity to become aware of the presence and action of God in their lives and in the world around them. Indeed God is not far from each one of us. For 'in him we live an move and have our being' (Acts 17:28).

Having thus focused and explored, an important stage in the learning process is that moment when a person is able to say 'this is what I learnt', 'this is how that affects me', 'this is what that means for me in my own life'. For very young children this expression must take many and varied forms. They can say it in words, draw it in pictures, act it out in a play, and sing it in a song. In the programme, one of the ways through which they will always be encouraged to express what they have learnt in a particular lesson is prayer. Where appropriate, in line with the capacity of a child of this age, they are also encouraged to respond in an action, which shows that there are implications in what they have learnt for the way in which they live their lives.

At the senior end of the primary school, *Alive-O 5 – Alive-O 8*, the programme does not mention the process of *Focus, Explore* and *Respond*. Here, in the senior classes, the fundamental tasks of catechesis as outlined in the *General Directory for Catechesis* are given prominence.[7] These tasks are listed as promoting knowledge of the faith, liturgical education, moral formation, teaching to pray, education for community life and missionary initiation.

In presenting *doctrine*, it is important to stress the central truths of faith in order to achieve a proper perspective. Catechesis at all levels must take account of the most important truths of faith. These central truths of faith are highlighted in the *Alive-O* programme. However, they are presented in a manner suited to the age and faith development of primary schoolchildren.

Catechesis prepares the Christian to live in community and to participate actively in the life and mission of the Church. Parents, priests and teachers play a significant role in the *liturgical and sacramental initiation* of children. The experience of parish liturgy and the practice of parents and of the Christian community are vital elements for the liturgical and sacramental formation of children. Without these, little can be achieved at school. The *Alive-O* programme continues to introduce the children to the riches of the sacramental life of the Church. In the senior classes particular emphasis is placed on the Eucharist, the sacrament of Reconciliation and on the sacrament of Confirmation.

Christian *moral education* must bear in mind certain truths of Christian Revelation: our exalted destiny and vocation in Jesus Christ, the consequences of original and personal sin, our need for salvation, Christ's saving activity in his life, death and resurrection, and God's graceful presence and assistance. Therefore, Christian moral education includes teaching children to love and worship God and to live moral lives as a response to God's love. It involves developing in them an awareness of sin and a sense of penance. It also includes teaching them to follow and imitate Jesus Christ in his love of God and of all people, in his forgiveness of others and in his endurance in suffering. Moreover, it involves bringing them to an awareness of the role of the Holy Spirit, of prayer and of the sacraments in their efforts to overcome evil and sin and to live as children of God. Throughout the *Alive-O* programme the children are helped to become aware of God's love for us, manifested in the world around us and in the covenant with Abraham and Moses, and revealed fully in his Son, Jesus Christ. They are helped to appreciate that the life of the Christian should be a response of love to God, who first loved us. They are encouraged to realise that 'the gift of the Commandments and of the Law is part of the covenant God sealed with his own.'[8]

The *Alive-O* programme gives *prayer* a central place. The children's faith in God is fostered through prayer and they can learn to express this faith in prayer. Teaching children to pray is not the same as teaching definitions of prayer, nor is it as simple as teaching prayer formulas – though this is also important and is accommodated in the programme. All of the formal prayers mentioned in the *Religious Education Syllabus for Catholic Children in Primary Schools* are taught to the children on a progressive and repetitive basis. The children are also introduced to the three major forms of prayer in the Christian tradition namely vocal, meditative and contemplative prayer. The *Alive-O* programme lives and breathes in an atmosphere of prayer and opportunities for prayer are offered to the children on a regular basis.

In *Alive-O* the children focus on their belonging to the Church in the context of an understanding of the Church as a global and *Catholic community*. Throughout the programme children experience community in various ways. Both family and parish experiences can be powerful media for encountering and deepening a sense of community. In school, group class and whole school activities foster a sense of community and children are also encouraged to reach out to others, particularly to the marginalized. As a class children are also given opportunities during the duration of the programme to prepare for and celebrate the sacraments of Reconciliation, Eucharist and Confirmation, where appropriate.

The Church 'exists in order to evangelise', that is, 'the carrying forth of the Good News to every sector of the human race so that by its strength it may enter into the hearts of people and renew the human race.'[9] The *missionary* mandate of Jesus to evangelise has various aspects, all of which, however, are closely connected with one another: 'proclaim' (Mark 16:15), 'make disciples and teach', 'be my witnesses', 'baptise', 'do this in memory of me' (Luke 22:19), 'love one another' (John 15:12). All of these aspects of proclamation, witness, teaching, sacraments and love of neighbour are the means by which the one Gospel is transmitted and they constitute the essential elements of evangelisation itself. The *Alive-O* programme seeks to fulfil this task in co-operation with home and parish while being mindful of the age, stage of development and cultural context of the children to whom it is addressed.[10]

Notes

1. John Paul II, *Catechesi Tradendae,* Eng. trans. (Middlegreen: St Paul Publications, 1979), par. 17.
2. See *Catechismus Catholicae Ecclesiae* (1992), trans. Veritas *Catechism of the Catholic Church* (Dublin: Veritas, 1994).
3. See Congregation for the Clergy, *General Directory for Catechesis* (Dublin: Veritas, 1998).
4. See Irish Episcopal Commission on Catechetics, *Alive-O* (Dublin: Veritas, 1996-2003).
5. Kennedy, M. *Islands Apart* (Dublin: Veritas, 2000), p. 3.
6. Congregation for the Clergy, *General Directory for Catechesis*, par. 197.
7. Congregation for the Clergy, *General Directory for Catechesis*, pars. 85,86.
8. *Catechism of the Catholic Church*, par. 2060.
9. Paul VI, *Evangelii Nuntiandi,* Eng. trans. (Dublin: Veritas, 1975), pars. 14,18.
10. An earlier draft of this article appeared in *Religion, Education and the Arts* 4 (2003), pp. 13-20.

AWAKENING CHILDREN TO NEW WAYS OF SEEING THE WORLD

Re-telling the Parables of Jesus

Gerry O'Connell

In the *Alive-O* religious education programme Luke's version of the parable of the Lost Sheep (Luke 15:3-6) has replaced the story of Zacchaeus as the gospel story central to the liturgy for first Confession. In the First Class Programme (*Alive-O 3*) it has been adapted for the children to enable them to explore their experience of being lost and being found again. In the Second Class Programme (*Alive-O 4*) it is used as a basis for reflection on the children's experience of straying from God and from the community of others. The art suggested in this programme allows the children to work with their experience of separation, loss and searching, and with their need to be found.[1]

On one occasion, having read and pondered the parable of the Lost Sheep, the children in my class went on to express some aspect of it in art. One child began to talk to me about his picture. The picture contained three sheep – Mammy Sheep, Daddy Sheep and Baby Sheep. Mammy Sheep in an enclosed garden and Daddy Sheep on top of a steep hill were separated by a gate that, in the child's words, was too big. 'I couldn't make it any smaller,' he said, 'I tried.' Baby Sheep was climbing up the slope to try to see what Daddy Sheep was doing. That child talked and talked and talked about the picture. It was a picture of his own life and a portrayal of how he saw his home situation. For me it demonstrated the power of the parables of Jesus at work today, even in the case of young children.

This article begins with a brief re-imagining of the parable in the ministry of Jesus. It explores how parables work. It then considers the use of parables in *Alive-O* generally, and specifically the parable of the Lost Sheep for those engaged in first Confession and first Communion class. Finally its aim is to encourage the kind of restraint that Jesus' parables require in order to retain and realise their power.

What About Jesus and His Parables?

Jesus ministered to his own people throughout Palestine some two millennia ago by way of healing, table-fellowship, preaching and storytelling. The crowds that followed him came not for the sermons or the stories but for healing. Those who were healed were no longer considered excluded from the covenant community. For them the parables may simply have been clever table talk, asides, riddles or retorts. Jesus was not crucified for his parables, although he may have been crucified for the praxis they seemed to encourage. Whatever about all this, it is clear to us today that when the early Christians gathered and recorded their collective memories of the life of Jesus, the parables (in the case of the synoptic Gospels, Matthew, Mark and Luke) and the images they contain (in the case of John) had an important role to play.

Jesus, whose background was an oral culture marinated in Old Testament narrative, was a teller of parables. His concerns flowed from the Hebrew Scriptures, not from politics or history, nor from Greece or Rome. The connections between his parables and Old Testament stories provide further evidence of this. The parables of Jesus are rooted in and are a product of his socio-religious background. He used them to explode the myth that society was as God wanted it to be. That is what parables set out to achieve. They take the myths by which we explain our world and turn them on their head, inviting us to think again.

Through Jesus, God speaks and acts anew, announcing good news for the poor, liberty for captives and recovery of sight for the blind (Luke 4:18-19). Jesus sets up a paradigm of discipleship. He establishes a praxis that undermines the other 'gods' people esteem, such as money, status, and power, which in the end only enslave. The parables of Jesus are an occasion for dialogue. Jesus took risks in offering them in such a way as to lead his audience into a new way of seeing, a new way of hearing, a new way of doing. Jesus struggled to illuminate His hearers' understanding of the reign of God. He used parable as an experiential bridge through the imagination to the heart. Jesus announced the coming of the Kingdom by his actions as well as by his words. He not only proclaimed the message of the parables but he lived it and embodied it in his own person. His table-fellowship with sinners led to the Pharisees' murmurings, which in turn were the provocation for Luke's parable of the Lost Sheep (Luke 15:1-7).

The parables enabled Jesus to break through the expectations current in His day and bring about new understandings of the reign of God. In them he expressed what the coming Kingdom would be like. He suggested what kind of community God's reign could bring about, and how such developments were consistent with Yahweh's nature and actions as revealed to the Chosen People. This involved him in describing something significantly new and beyond the experience of those in his own society. And this is where the parable came into its own.

The parables of Jesus appeal to and are addressed to more than just the mind; for the reign of God cannot be summed up in words. They are also addressed to the heart with the intention of evoking an affective response. In parables, Jesus represents the values and resources of Yahweh penetrating the conscious and unconscious experience of his listeners; they enable him to break through the conventions and expectations of his day and to bring the reign of God alive in the experience of those who listen:

> One of the most certain facts from the life of Jesus is that he expressed the reality of God as he saw it through his message of the kingdom of God and his action in accordance with it, personally in a very special and distinctive way. He made clear the content of this message, about the God who loves humanity, by means of his parables, in which conversion and alternative possibilities of life are offered: the praxis of the kingdom of God.[2]

The parables are powerful stories that come alive when taken to heart. These parables of Jesus work gently, but forcefully, inviting the hearer to look again at how society is organised:

> Parables give God room. The parables of Jesus are *not* historical allegories telling us how God acts with mankind; neither are they moral example-stories telling us how to act before God and towards one another. They are stories, which shatter the deep structure of our accepted world and thereby render clear and evident to us the relativity of story itself. They remove our defences and make us vulnerable to God. It is only in such

experiences that God can touch us and only in such moments does the kingdom of God arrive.[3]

Jesus proclaimed the good news of the coming reign of God in a manner befitting his audience and an oral culture. His audience was empowered to move the parable from head to heart to hand, from hearing to taking it to heart to becoming disciples, from metaphor to dialogue to praxis. Even though the world of Jesus was confined, his imagination was not limited by that confinement. Jesus said things in parables that could not be said so well in prose. The following poem written by scripture scholar Tom Hamill in his own unique style illustrates this point:

The Reign Of God Its Hinted Likenesses
Like a treasure hidden, whispers 'find-me'!
Like a baker woman, lavishes bread!
Like a glowing pearl, yearns my-skin!
Like a sower of seed, trusts the ground!
Like a wedding feast, discourages none!
Like a tiny weed, leaps & spreads!
Like a precious vineyard, suffers force!
Like a good shepherd, seeks the stray!
Like a well made net, encompasses all![4]

What about *Alive-O* and the Lost Sheep?
The *Alive-O* Programme recognises the importance of storytelling and includes stories in every lesson, pointing out that in the Christian tradition this is not an innovation:

> Jesus told stories that challenged the people of his day to look again at their experiences. Through his stories he

challenged them to re-evaluate these in the light of the values of God's kingdom, which he explored in concrete terms in his stories.[5]

Just as Zacchaeus was lodged in the mindset of a generation of children as an example of God's forgiveness, love and table-fellowship with all, so the parable of the Lost Sheep will, likewise for the current generation, provide an abiding image of God as the One who searches for those who stray.

The parable appears in both Luke and Matthew, and also the gnostic Gospel of Thomas. In Luke's version Jesus uses it to answer the murmurings of the Pharisees regarding his table-fellowship with sinners. It was then transformed by the primitive Church into a pastoral exhortation not to stray from the community, as in Matthew's version. In the Gospel of Thomas, the emphasis is on the shepherd who goes to look for the lost sheep because it is the greatest or the most valuable one of them all. The whole point in this parable seems to be the risk involved, leaving the ninety-nine to look for the one. Matthew emphasises seeking, Luke the joy of finding. The parable and the action of Jesus around it manifest an implicit theology, namely that Jesus acts on God's behalf, as God's representative. This in turn allows an insight into Jesus' own self-understanding. The parable of the Lost Sheep illustrates the single-mindedness required of those who seek the kingdom of God. A similar single-mindedness is to be seen in the parables of the Treasure and of the Pearl.

The parable of the Lost Sheep is a similitude. This is the most concise type of parable. It briefly narrates a typical event from real life. It gains its persuasiveness by recounting what is widely recognised as true. In the case of the similitude of the Lost Sheep none of the listeners would deny the truth of the story. One of the most notable things about the world of parables is that it is not the ideal world, the 'nice' world. Nor is it a 'refurbished', 'tidied' world. It recounts a thoroughly 'temporal' world where nothing is sugar-coated and where 'experiences of the world' correspond to the real world of Jesus' time. In the parable of the Lost Sheep, a shepherd, not an angel of God, finds the lost sheep. For some people at that time, such as contemporary historian Philo, there was no more disreputable occupation than that of a shepherd.[6] It can be seen therefore, that there is no attempt to make this blemished world a little bit more 'whole' – as one might expect when drawing a comparison with the kingdom of God. It is helpful then, when using parables to be aware of their connection to everyday life at the time they were told.

Clearly, within the *Alive-O* series parables are not merely presented as a didactic exercise or for analysis as if they have no effect in people's lives. In the story 'Lost and Found' in *Alive-O 4*, the parables of the Lost Coin, Lost Sheep, Yeast, Sower and Lamp have been combined in one story and brought to life in drama. In *Alive-O 6*, the children are given the opportunity to explore, the parable of the Prodigal Son modified for today's Fourth Class audience, through drama. The presentation of these stories in drama brings them to life and in this form become, as Tom Groome says, 'a powerful way to both engage and invite people's souls to expression.'[7] Prayer and art are recommended by *Alive-O* as further ways of opening up imaginative and reflective work with children. The approach of Sofia Cavalletti comes to mind in her 'Catechesis of the Good Shepherd'[8] as does the 'Godly Play' workshops of Jerome Berryman. In his book *Godly Play*, Jerome Berryman outlines a case study entitled 'Two Boys and a Parable'[9]. Here he recounts how two boys interacted with parable over a period of twelve

Saturday workshops. One day, one of the boys, Jimmy, decided to work through the medium of paint. When Berryman came to look at the painting, Jimmy pointed something out and said, 'These little things are the parables. No, they are the pearls.' Is that what the parables are? Or is that what they have the potential to be? Jimmy's slip of the tongue makes for a very interesting reflection.

What About Parables and Teaching?

To listen to the Parables of Jesus, it seems to me, is to let one's imagination be opened to the new possibilities disclosed by the extravagance of these short dramas. If we look at the parables as at a word addressed first to our imagination rather than to our will, we shall not be tempted to reduce them to mere didactic devices, to moralizing allegories. We will let their poetic power display itself within us ... Poetic means more than poetry as a literary genre. Poetic means creative. And it is in the heart of our imagination that we let the event happen, before we may convert our heart and tighten our will.[10]

Jesus had a listening heart that enabled Him, through His imagination, to respond empathically to people. He told his parables to an orally-conscious Jewish audience. The early Church remembered, modified and retold the parables to its listeners. While it is impossible for us to be in exactly the same position as the people to whom Jesus actually spoke, we too, nevertheless remember his stories, modify them and re-tell them today. In this way his parables are heard again and brought to life. Through the re-telling of the parables, Jesus speaks again today. The parables have the power to touch our hearts. They invite us to think again, to sense the wonder and to reshape our actions.

Benedictine Mark Patrick Hederman writes: 'We can stop the world and redirect it, if we have sufficient understanding and imagination both to point out the better way and make it compelling enough to accomplish.'[11] Will those who work with *Alive-O* be able to subvert the myth that post-Celtic-Tiger Ireland is as Jesus would want it to be? What does the parable of the Lost Sheep say to us today about separation and loss, seeking and finding, and the possibility of a whole new way of contemplating the world we inhabit. Jesus not only told parables but engaged in parabolic behaviour. Can teachers do the same? Could lunchtime be seized on for table-fellowship? Could the classroom become a place of healing where, for example, those who are hurt might have their stories listened to? Might teaching become parabolic, setting our comfortable world on its head and, under the tender gaze of the Good Shepherd, open us up to the life of unconditional love proclaimed by Jesus as central to the reign of God?

Notes

1. See for example, E. Gormally, M. Hyland and C. Maloney *Alive-O 4, Teacher's Book* (Dublin: Veritas, 1999), pp. 224-236.
2. E. Schillebeeckx, *The Church with a Human Face: A New and Expanded Theology of Ministry*, trans. J. Bowden (London: SCM, 1985), p. 23.
3. J.D. Crossan, *The Dark Interval: Towards a Theology of Story*, (Niles, Illinois: Argus, 1975), pp. 121-122.
4. *Armagh Diocesan Biblical Initiative*, Sunday 28 July 2002: Ordinary Time: A [online]. Available from http://www.adbi.net/
5. C. Maloney, F. O'Connell and B. O'Reilly, *Alive-O 7, Teacher's Book* (Dublin: Veritas, 2003), p. [29].
6. See 'Philo de agric. 61', cited in J. Jeremias, *Jerusalem in the Time of Jesus*, trans. F.H. and C.H. Cave (London: SCM, 1969), p. 311.
7. T.H. Groome, *Educating For Life: A Spiritual Vision for Every Teacher and Parent* (1998), paperback edition (New York: Crossroad, 2001), p. 352.
8. See S. Cavalletti, *The Religious Potential of the Child*, (1979), trans. Missionary Society of St. Paul (New York: Paulist Press, 1983), pp. 65-76.
9. See J.W. Berryman, *Godly Play: An Imaginative Approach to Religious Education* (1991), reprinted (San Francisco: Harper, 1995), pp. 45-60.
10. P. Ricoeur, 'Listening to the Parables of Jesus', C.E. Reagan and D. Stewart (eds.) *The Philosophy of Paul Ricoeur: An Anthology of His Work* (Boston: Beacon Press, 1978), p. 245.
11. M.P. Hederman, *The Haunted Inkwell: Art and Our Future* (Dublin: Columba, 2001), p. 34.

ABOARD HOGWARTS EXPRESS

Harry Potter in the Religion Class?

Joe Collins

There's a mystery afoot in the publishing industry. It started in 1997 when an unknown and struggling Scottish author wrote a children's book called *Harry Potter and the Philosopher's Stone*. Ever since J.K. Rowling first penned the words 'Harry Potter', it has become a truly remarkable phenomenon. The statistics alone are staggering. Harry Potter's magic has touched a huge audience of all ages all over the world. In America, there are nearly 80 million books in print, and each title has been on *The New York Times*, *USA Today* and *Wall Street Journal* bestseller lists. The fifth title, *Harry Potter and the Order of the Phoenix*, broke all records with its first print run of 6.8 million copies and a second print run of an additional 1.7 million copies, a figure unprecedented for any book.[1] J. K. Rowling has won the Hugo Award, the Bram Stoker Award, the Whitbread Award for Best Children's Book, a special commendation for the Anne Spencer Lindbergh Prize, and a special certificate for being a three-year winner of the Smarties Prize, as well as many other honours. Rowling has also been named an Officer of the British Empire.

With over a quarter of a billion copies sold, the books have been translated into sixty-one languages and distributed in over two hundred countries. All five books have become bestsellers in the United States, Britain and around the globe. The Harry Potter phenomenon helped publisher Bloomsbury to record huge rises in profits; making J.K. Rowling, according to the 2003 Forbes list, a billionaire.[2]

It raises the question – is the Harry Potter phenomenon just a passing fad or is there is something more fundamental at play here? Stripped to its basics, the whole Harry Potter business is about one thing essentially: it is about story!

The stories of Harry Potter have become so much a part of the lives of so many of the children sitting in classrooms that the teacher needs to enquire how this might be used to good effect in regard to the education of children. In this respect, religious education is no exception. Indeed, because religion itself, including Christianity, relies so much on story, it is very desirable that primary school educators take time to consider how something like the Harry Potter phenomenon might be utilised in developing and nurturing the faith life of the young. Such is the purpose of this article, which sets itself the following tasks:

- It will explore the nature of children's religious faith
- It will look at the nature of story in human experience
- It will enquire as to how story may assist in faith development
- It will consider the potential of the Harry Potter corpus for Religious Education
- It will reflect on the challenge and invitation this presents to the teacher
- And finally come to some conclusions about the use of story in faith development.

Children's Religious Faith

The *Alive-O* programme, just like the *Children of God Series* before it, notes that 'The aim of Religious Education is to foster and deepen the children's faith.'[3] In seeking to understand and gain some appreciation of the faith life of children, it is worthwhile visiting the work of developmental psychologist, James Fowler. He perceives faith as a universal human quest for meaning through which people attempt to make sense of their existence. While faith is more commonly expressed, according to Fowler, through unique and different religious traditions, it is not necessarily to be understood exclusively as a religious concept for the reason that it transcends many boundaries. Faith, he maintains, finds its source in human interpersonal relationships, where humans reach out in trust to others in an agreeable and an embracing way. Hence, the self only comes to faith through relationship with another. However, any relationship is incomplete unless it is of a triadic nature incorporating a third element. This element is referred to by Fowler as the 'ultimate environment' by which is understood 'a centre of value and power adequate to ground, unify, and order the whole force-field of life.'[4] In Judaeo-Christian terms this is expressed as the 'Kingdom of God' or 'Reign of God' where divinity functions as the centre of power and value, unifying and giving character to the ultimate environment. For Fowler then, faith offers a path along which one is guided and encouraged and where one can always maintain hope of nurturing personal realities.

Fowler outlined six stages of faith. However, the most relevant of these stages to this article is Stage 2, *Mythical-Literal Faith* (childhood and beyond): 'Where the developing ability to think logically helps one to order the world with categories of causality, space and time; to enter into perspectives of others; and to capture life meaning in stories.[5] In respect of children's religious faith this means that story sharing, whether of culture or of the sacred type, is part of a total conventional reality. The mystery of story is that everyone is one and everyone has some. In a suitable setting everyone wants to tell stories. Without stories, there is no knowledge of the world, of ourselves, or of God.

The Nature of Story in Human Experience

As a prelude to dealing with story in respect of faith-development, mention must be given to the function of story in human experience in general. Stories have always appealed to young children and still retain their popularity. Storytelling has been around since the earliest days of communication and the themes, responses, character types and actions have been refined by acceptability through time. Many of the themes common to books of fiction are calculated to appeal naturally to children. The stories often contain sufferings but also the eventual triumph of the small, the weak, and even the stupid while at the same time fun is often directed at authority. These stories usually contain a lot of humour, as they deal with role and fortune reversals while eliciting the sympathies of the reader in favour of the trickster who wins by breaking all the rules. Neither are cruelty, fear and death avoided as these are necessary parts of human existence.

While there is much entertainment to be wrought from storytelling, it also provides an opportunity to discuss more serious issues with children. These may include a discussion of goodness and why and how one should be good, of repentance and fear, and of a whole range of other moral issues such as the humiliation of others and of winning through cheating. But to over-moralise or to over-extract meaning from some of these children's books can render the exercise null and void. Stories can bond hearer to narrator, opening up new vistas, expanding horizons, challenging, affirming, soothing and comforting. Above all, stories can reveal to men, women and children especially, insights into worlds never experienced or imagined, and enable them to bridge the known and the unknown.

The Role of Story in Faith Development

Faith has to do with worlds not seen by human eyes yet apprehended by human hearts. Stories can be the vehicles to transport the child between these two realities where they encounter good and bad, challenge and commitment, justice and cheating. Fowler views storytelling as central to faith because it provides 'effective ways for children to externalise their inner anxieties and to find ordering images and stories by which to begin to shape their lives.'[6]

The growing awareness of the role of narratives is evident here. Not alone do stories act as a tool of communication for children but also the children, as listeners, can recreate meaning from the events symbolised. Stories can be employed to entertain, to preserve a culture, to socialise, to draw morals or to help someone reorganise experience therapeutically. While much of the content of story confirms previously held attitudes and beliefs, it can also challenge these values and possibly even change them.

The educative value of a good story lies partly in the fact that it holds up a mirror to life and in the fact that it enables children to contemplate experiences by proxy. Story can enrich the imagination; provide a kind of escape-therapy needed at times in human life; develop compassion, humour and understanding; arouse curiosity as well as the ability to question the particular thought-systems humans inherit; and furnish the joy and satisfaction resulting from personal awareness.

The Potential of the Harry Potter Corpus for Religious Education

Many teachers wonder how the Harry Potter books can best serve the needs of education. In this regard, Christian religious educators are no exception. In endeavouring to find an answer to this question interviews were set for six children, three boys and three girls, from fifth and sixth classes on topics such as God and faith. The children's answers to the questions posed were, in most cases, very insightful and indicative of their reflection upon the elements of the faith that had been passed on to them through one channel or another. In terms of findings from the research there were anthropomorphic elements in many of the children's images of God (a man with a beard and blue eyes). They perceived God's actions as being justified and did not see them as reciprocals of God's wrath on his people when they are poor and unfortunate. Abstract concepts, such as the omnipresence of God and the afterlife, were expressed creatively by the children.

Once collated, the responses of the children, indicated where they were at in terms of faith and how children structure meaning. This provided an opportunity to introduce stories from the Harry Potter series to the whole group, comprising fifth and sixth classes together, and to pitch the stories, as appropriate, at their faith stage. Here the interviewer tried to pick up on the observations gleaned from the interviews. As a result a number of insights emerged.

There was an overwhelmingly positive response from the children to follow-up activities in the classroom. Through a combination of narration and discussion, life's meaning as manifested in the themes from the Harry Potter stories was explored and the children's imaginations cultivated. Through the explorations, the children drew connections with other curricular areas and indeed with extra-curricular areas also. Despite the pre-arranged activities that followed each narration, the stories leant themselves to alternate multi-dimensional approaches, opening up unending possibilities for the children and their faith development. The interviews with the six children, provided a useful means of ascertaining the children's understanding of explicit matters of faith. The real faith development was to be seen, however, both in the children's reactions to the Harry Potter stories and in the way that the story interpretations were personalised.

Challenges for the Teacher

Education must be attentive to the questions and assumptions of children. It must begin from where the children are at and incorporate their language into classroom discourse. Accordingly, there is need for teachers to keep in touch with the culture of children as a necessary step in helping to bridge the worlds of the seen and the unseen, the human and the divine, the secular and the religious.

In addition, it is extremely important for the teacher of religion to assist children in seeking and finding the good and God in stories that attract and hold their attention. This requires developing question and discussion strategies to help the children discover, penetrate, and make meaning out of the mystery of life.

The Harry Potter series, used judiciously, has potential for engaging senior primary school children with various aspects of the Christian faith. Faith is a lifetime process. Story at any age is an essential ingredient within this continuum and should always be encouraged in the educational field. While there are many audio-visual presentations and adaptations of the Harry Potter series available, teachers would be well advised to read or, better still, tell the stories to the children. The reason for this lies in the unique role played by the storyteller, who acts as the human intermediary between the fantastical world and the real world. It is important to allow the children to interpret the story in whatever way they see fit respecting the particular stage of faith development they may presently be at.

Teachers of religion also need to be aware of discussions relating to the spiritual dimension of the Harry Potter books, evidenced by a growing literature in this area.[7] The Christian community, particularly in the United States, has been embroiled in a heated debate between those who assert that the Harry Potter books are an attempt to popularise occult practices and those who see the stories as fantasy, in line with the age-old tradition of children's literature. The anti-Harry Potter sentiment became so strong, at one point, that it sparked a whole series of book-burnings by some Christians.[8] Even though this is an extreme occurrence, it has tended to monopolise almost any mention of Christianity in relation to the Harry Potter literature. At a personal and professional level, it was a fascination with this negative publicity, in addition to a curiosity as to the huge interest and enjoyment that children seemed to be deriving from these books, that led me to wonder about and explore their value.

A Literary Miracle

The children currently in primary school are commonly referred to as the 'PlayStation Generation' who happily while away the hours with a keyboard mouse or a television remote control. The perception is that they are hardly likely to be seen with their noses buried in a book. The fact, however, that they hunger vociferously to read about Harry Potter is judged to be nothing short of a minor literary miracle. The fact that the

Potter books, with their male protagonist and the author's androgynous byline, appeals to boys is seen as a bonus. During the course of the research one teacher commentated that the Harry Potter books are a marvelous addition to children's literature, because they get the children reading and talking about books per se. A by-product of this, in the eyes of many teachers, is the enhancement of classroom discussion and learning throughout the entire curriculum.

Conclusion

The Harry Potter corpus deals clearly with the themes of good versus evil and with the fantasy world of magic. There exists a deep human need to step out of the everyday and to create an alternative place in which human imagination can wander about freely. Through this imaginary world children can resolve some of the moral dilemmas that cannot easily be tested in the world of the everyday. Part of the genius of J.K. Rowling lies in her ability to construct a world that allows children to identify with characters and situations in such a way that these vital developmental tasks are carried out. An overriding challenge for religious educators therefore consists in enabling children to exercise their imaginations to know God's world and, ultimately, to know God.

Faith, of its very nature, transcends all subject boundaries and affects the whole school ethos. Story is a vital teaching and learning tool in the faith life of children. There is no more useful element for the teacher than that of story for entering into the mindset of the child and for encouraging a fertile understanding of life. Accordingly, it can be claimed that initiation into faith should incorporate story with concept. Education must be open to the modern world. The culture of the child includes books such as the Harry Potter series.

Through an exploration of stories similar to those found here, faith finds a contemporary cultural voice enabling the child to recognise both good and evil in stories and, subsequently, in their lives. What the Harry Potter phenomenon shows us is that the use of story from popular culture can serve as an important tool in religious faith development.

Notes

1. See http://www.scholastic.com/harrypotter/author [Accessed 29 June, 2004].
2. See http://www.bomis.com/rings/Nharry_potter_series-articles_and_interviews-arts [Accessed 29 June, 2004].
3. P. O'Reilly and C. Maloney, *Alive-O 6, Teacher's Book,* (Dublin: Veritas, 2002), p. [12].
4. J.W. Fowler, 'Faith and the Structuring of Meaning', C. Brusselmans, (ed.) *Toward Moral and Religious Maturity. The First International Conference on Moral and Religious Development* (Morristown: Silver Burdett Company, 1980), p. 56.
5. J.W. Fowler, 'The Vocation of Faith Development Theory', J.W. Fowler, K.E. Nipkow and F. Schweitzer (eds.) *Stages of Faith and Religious Development: Implications for Church, Education and Society,* (Centre for Research in Faith and Moral Development, Candler School of Theology, Emory University: SCM Press, 1991), p. 24.
6. J.W. Fowler, *Stages of Faith: The Psychology of Human Development and the Quest for Meaning,* (San Francisco: Harper, 1981), p. 130.
7. See R. Abanes, *Harry Potter and the Bible: The Menace Behind the Magic* (Camp Hill, PA: Horizon Books, 2001); F. Bridger, *A Charmed Life: The Spirituality of Potterworld* (London: Darton, Longman & Todd, 2001); J. Houghton, *A Closer Look at Harry Potter: Bending and Shaping the Minds of Our Children* (Eastbourne: Kingsway, 2001); C. Neal, *The Gospel According to Harry Potter* (Louisville, Kentucky: John Knox Press, 2001); C. Neal, *What's a Christian to Do with Harry Potter?* (New York: Waterbrook Press, 2001).
8. For information regarding book burnings see http://www.cbn.com and other websites.

STRATEGY FOR EFFECTIVE USE OF STORY IN TEACHING

Michael Hayes

C.S. Lewis, the noted medieval scholar and author of the famous Narnia books, was regarded with suspicion by certain of his fellow academics when he first began to write his science-fiction trilogy. It was felt by some that by so doing he was cheapening his talent and learning. Lewis himself strongly defended what he was doing and was quite insistent that story should be celebrated for itself. He saw it as having a value of its own. That the great stories are timeless is a point he wished to make: 'No book is worth reading at the age of ten,' he claimed, 'which is not equally (and often far more) worth reading at the age of fifty. The only imaginative works we ought to grow out of are those which it would have been better not to have read at all.'[1]

Renowned Irish philosopher, Richard Kearney, also recognises the importance of story. He stresses that we can only become agents of our own history when we transform haphazard happenings into narrative. This is as true on the communal level as it is on the individual level . We tell our story in order to transform time from the impersonal passing of fragmented moments into a pattern, a history. For Kearney, every story, in every genre, has a common function of someone telling something to someone about something or other. Whoever was the first to say, 'Once upon a time,' lit bonfires in the imaginations of listeners. Taking a leaf out of Socrates' book, Kearney suggests that 'the unnarrated life is not worth living'.[2]

The purpose of this article is to ask whether the full potential of story is being realised in the classroom. As teachers, are we simply content just to read or tell the story without exploring its deeper life-giving value? Even if we do use story, do we try to move beyond it as entertainment to story as education for living? This article attempts to show how story might be used in such a way, and to explore particularly how it may benefit the teaching of religion. An illustration will help to make this point.

The Story of Gelert the Hound

There is an old Welsh folk tale from the thirteenth century about a hunting hound. Gelert was Prince Llewelyn's favourite hound, the best hunting dog in Wales. He ate at the prince's table and guarded his bed at night. The prince never hunted without Gelert. One day the prince's friends called for him to go on the hunt. Seeing that the day was good, he blew on his hunting horn to call the hounds. All of his hounds answered the call except Gelert. He called again for Gelert to come. When the hound failed to come, the prince irritably headed off on the hunt without him.

Even though the conditions were good, the hunt was not as successful as usual because of Gelert's absence. When Prince Llewelyn returned to his home that evening, his humour had not improved. As he neared the gate he saw Gelert bounding out to meet him. Seeing blood dripping from the hound's lips, Llewelyn suddenly realised that in his haste to join the hunt, he had left his infant son unattended. On running to the child's room, he saw the cradle overturned and no sign of the boy. The walls were spattered with blood and the child's blanket was torn and wet with blood. Concluding that Gelert had killed the baby, the prince fiercely turned on the hound, which had followed him in, and thrust his sword into his side. Gelert fell dying at his master's feet, gazing up at him in sadness, shock and surprise.

The dying groan of the hound woke the sleeping child, who had been hidden behind the overturned cradle. Prince Llewelyn rushed to the darkened corner of the room, and not only did he find his son unharmed and smiling up at him, but he also saw the dead body of a large wolf. His relief on finding the child alive was soon replaced by horror as he realised his error: Gelert had stayed behind from the hunt to guard the cradle and had fought and killed the wolf that had tried to attack the sleeping child. And Llewelyn had rewarded the hound's loyalty with death! Filled with remorse, he rushed back to where Gelert had fallen. It was too late. Gelert was already dead. Llewelyn's remorse was such that he never smiled again. He built a tomb for his brave hound, and the town that now stands at the place is called Beddgelert, the grave of Gelert.

This story, of which there are several versions, has fascinated audiences for generations. In some the gory battle between Gelert and the huge wolf is detailed. Others emphasise the regret and helplessness of the prince at the end of the story. Whatever about the historical truth of the legend, the impact which it has on new listeners is always real. Some are silent, almost stunned by the brutality of the ending. Those who do respond usually do so along the lines of 'Why didn't he check first before he killed the dog?' Invariably, the responses show that the children comprehend Llewelyn's tragedy and share it vicariously.

Like all great stories, the story of Gelert the Hound touches on universal truth and on themes such as love and loyalty, trust and betrayal, impulsive action and regret. Some of the story is probably factual, but it has no doubt been embellished in the telling and retelling. Through the power of this story, all listeners can share in Llewelyn's predicament, and recognise that they too could, and do, make similar mistakes. Like Llewelyn, they are susceptible to arriving at the wrong conclusions, at making erroneous judgements. Why? The answer is simple: because like Llewelyn, many often make hasty unsubstantiated judgements, failing in the process to assemble the evidence and check the facts.

Children's instinctive responses to the story show something of which we are all aware. They know, as Llewelyn painfully knew, that his tragedy was the result of failing to see the whole picture before acting. His failure to grasp all the evidence led to his developing a false understanding. This in turn led to his acting with such disastrous consequences.

The original narrator of Gelert's tale, in all probability, never intended that it would be dissected in this way. Its impact and survival as an enthralling tale after eight hundred years, is due to the fact that it connects with a truth that all instinctively sense. No teacher has to explain to a child who is hearing the story for the first time why it is so sad and tragic. The reason for this is that the author of Gelert's tale connects with something deep within all humans.

Hearers of the tale, if given a choice, might be inclined to suggest a more palatable happy ever-after ending along the following lines: Llewelyn would arrive back from the hunt as before and would be met once again by Gelert. Horrified, as he is in the original version of the story, by the sight of blood dripping from the hound's jaws he would rush into the castle in search of his son and Gelert would follow him into the bloodstained room. Fearing that Gelert had killed the child, he would have his hand on his sword would be just about to use it, when, hoping for some further explanation, he would search the room thoroughly. On seeing the dead wolf and the sleeping child his fear would vanish and his anger turn to relief and joy. He would take the child in his arms and march outside proudly to tell his men of Gelert's heroic act. Everyone would rejoice and would live happily ever after, Llewelyn being remembered as a wise and just prince and his son growing up to be a great leader.

Such happy endings are the stuff of many a fairy tale. Through them, we want our children to feel they live in a secure world where, ultimately, good triumphs over evil. In *Snow White*, *Sleeping Beauty* and *Jack and the Beanstalk*, good triumphs over evil and everybody lives happily ever after. Such stories fit a paradigm of order. At a very simple level, humans seek order in the world, the triumph of cosmos over chaos. Fairy tales affirm this order. That they resolve tension and dissonance is why children demand to hear them again and again. Satisfied, the child can slip off to sleep knowing that all is well with the world.

A certain part of us would like all stories to have happy endings. However, life is not like that. Much of life does not end happily. Stories such as Llewelyn's reflect that. But they do more – they educate, they inform, they enlighten, they instruct, precisely to ensure that we are not the authors of our own tragedies as was poor Llewelyn. However, stories can only accomplish this if they are reflected upon and consequently acted upon. In order to truly teach, instruct and guide, they have to be engaged with at a level beyond that of entertainment. They must be seen not so much as instances for 'learning about', but as opportunities for 'learning from'. In order for this to occur, a teacher needs to possess and master a strategy for using story with children. The remainder of this article will outline and illustrate the use of such a strategy.

Using the Story to Effect

If we were allowed to travel back in time to warn Llewelyn, what might we tell him? Perhaps we could plan to arrive at the critical moment and shout our warning to him. But then there's the possibility we would be putting ourselves in danger by mysteriously materialising in front of an already agitated man with a sword in his hand. Even if we were successful in saving Gelert, who is to say that the impulsive Llewelyn might not have authored an even greater tragedy for himself the next day or at some point later in his life?

What Llewelyn requires is not a specific warning for that day, but the adoption of an attitude to life, an outlook or a disposition which will enable him to consistently act in a responsible way, and which will protect him from acting unreasonably and irresponsibly. Providentially, such a system exists. The story, in fact, hints at the life lessons to be learned. Let's look again at what led Llewelyn to make his tragic error:

> He saw the evidence that blood had been spilled;
> He understood (incorrectly) that the blood was his son's;
> And he decided to act in accordance with what he understood to be true.

This process led Llewelyn to act with tragic consequences. Obviously therefore, as a procedure, it is inadequate as it stands. How can it be improved so that Llewelyn can depend on it and trust in it to help him to act responsibly?

The alternative version of Gelert's tale was altered to fit this demand for harmony. In it, Llewelyn looked at the evidence and found one explanation for what he saw (i.e. that Gelert killed the baby). He rejected it as being an inadequate explanation when he checked and saw all of the evidence. He then replaced his false understanding with the correct one. This in turn led him to avoid the disastrous course of action, which he had been contemplating, and to act reasonably, in accordance with his correct interpretation of events.

In this altered version of the story, the one with the happy ending, one could say that Llewelyn acted in accordance with the maxim, 'look before you leap', in that he:

- Looked at all the evidence
- Organised and interpreted the evidence to form an understanding
- Checked his understanding against all the evidence, rejecting any conclusions that were not entirely in accord with the evidence
- And finally, he acted in a way that was proper in the circumstances.

It can be seen from this that such a process has four levels. What the tragic Llewelyn did not have in the first version was the part where the conclusion he reached was checked for accuracy. Without this checking level, or level of judgement, his manner of coming to know was flawed and incomplete and resulted in his acting impetuously. When this level is added to the process, Llewelyn's judgements are correct and he acts responsibly. Now, through the insertion of this 'safety-net,' there is in place a process which commences with experience, and moves on through understanding to judgement and finally to responsible action. If, somehow, Llewelyn had been aware of the four-stage process and had acted in accordance with it, the catastrophe could have been averted.

This four-stage process of coming to know and learn was identified by a Canadian philosopher-theologian, Bernard Lonergan. In his exploration of how the human mind works, Lonergan discovered that it is only by being consciously aware of this process in ourselves that we become authentic human knowers. For Lonergan, each part is essential to the process. One begins at the level of experience and attends to the data that is gathered by the senses. At this first stage, one needs to be selective regarding the data attended to. Otherwise there would be no filtering out of the irrelevant information and reorganisation of the significant data. The detective at the crime scene, gathering as much evidence as possible, illustrates this procedure very well.

Once we have so selected and organised the data we can try to understand it. Here the detective sifts through the collected evidence, discarding that which is not germane to the investigation and examining the rest more carefully, bringing intelligence into play. A number of 'leads' may develop at this stage as the detective tries to make sense of the information. There is a tension, which Lonergan calls the tension of inquiry. This is the stage where understanding occurs, and when it comes, the tension is broken with the 'Aha!' of insight.

If the process were to stop at this stage, there would be nothing to protect the enquirer from arriving at false understanding, such as occurs when the insight appears to match the data observed. Sense experience seems, for instance, to tell us that the world is flat. Llewelyn's 'insight' that Gelert had killed the baby seems equally as valid as the real story. If the goal of the cognitional process was simply insight, then we could say that the goal had been achieved and the process was complete. However, this does nothing for poor old Llewelyn. As he tragically and only later found out, he needed another level in the process of dealing with the situation. It was his ignorance of this level that produced the hasty and irrational action which ensued.

This third level then is the stage at which insights are tested for accuracy by checking them against the data which has been observed. Sometimes it is not easy to confirm which of the competing insights is the correct one. At the third level, as long as there is doubt about the insight, one cannot say that it has been fully understood. It was this level of judgement, which poor Llewelyn failed to avail of in the original story. In the 'corrected' alternative version, however, it was precisely his attention to and use of it that spared him from killing Gelert. It can be seen from this, therefore, that the level of judgement is crucial to the integrity of the process but that it only comes into play *after* the first two levels.

Once these three levels are dealt with one is ready to move on to the fourth level where Lonergan introduces the ethical or moral dimension. The first three stages focus on knowing while the fourth level is preoccupied with responsibility and decision. This is the level where the person, who knows the good, has the opportunity of deciding to do the good.

Lonergan's method, as outlined above, has universal applicability. It is based on the fact and reality that every conscious person can apprehend sense data, have insights, develop understanding and make judgements. His method can be applied to all fields of learning. The process is universal. Lonergan's theory is concerned with what Aristotle calls the 'urge to know' and which Lonergan himself calls the 'pure desire to know', which impels everyone through the process of coming to know. In summary then the four levels are:

- The Empirical (the level of apprehending the data of experience)
- The Intellectual (where one strives to understand, to make sense of the data)
- The Rational (where a judgement as to the accuracy of one's understanding is made) and
- The Responsible or Moral level (which involves acting on the judgements arrived at).

The first three levels of the structure all involve cognitional activity. Together they comprise a recurrent, continual process of attempting to make sense of the world. The activities engaged in at these levels are necessary functions for the acquisition of meaning. Performing all of these activities constitutes a scientific method. An illustration of this method in action sees the scientist observing a phenomenon, formulating a hypothesis to explain it, checking and evaluating the hypothesis, and finally, either confirming the hypothesis or formulating a new one.

The Educational Application of Lonergan's Theory

Lonergan's method is a tool that can be used in all areas of education, and can aid in the achievement of all of the specific aims of the *Primary School Curriculum* (1999). In particular, it assists in the achievement of the aim: 'to enable children to develop spiritual, moral and religious values.' It is capable of accomplishing this because it moves beyond the first three levels of consciousness to a fourth level, the level where these values are applied. The fourth level, the level of response, is a crucial part of the whole process. This is the level where decisions are made, and is essential to any programme of religious education which seeks to teach children 'to live moral lives as a response to God's love.'[3]

The Four Imperatives (The 'Must-Do's')

A person, who is consciously seeking to learn, must firstly be attentive, with all of their senses, to all the data at the Empirical level. Being intelligent at the second level requires that the person seek to understand the data of his or her sense experience. At the third level, being reasonable, the person checks all the possible alternative explanations, committing to one. Fourthly, being responsible, the person must act according to what they now know as true.

The Benefits of Using Lonergan's Theory

This article suggests Lonergan's cognitional theory as a method for effectively using story, 'one of our most viable forms of *identity* – individual and communal' as Kearney sees it.[4] In the process of developing identity, there are benefits for all involved in education. The teacher has a soundly based theory from which to develop the questioning techniques which will lead the students through the process. Learners benefit by being trained in a method that teaches them to 'look before leaping' and to test the veracity of conclusions before acting. Society in general benefits because the theory facilitates action based on truth rather than on hearsay, whim, bias or self-interest.

There are benefits also for religious education itself. The religious message is no longer something to be just listened to: it is something to be lived. By using a Lonerganian approach, the teacher will be able to create structures for religious education that will allow the children the opportunity to move between all four levels of consciousness, and by so doing, move beyond the levels of knowing to the level of doing. J.R.R. Tolkien, whose masterpiece *The Lord of the Rings* has found a whole new audience thanks to the power of cinematic technology to re-present and re-tell story, once shared the following with C.S. Lewis:

> We have come from God, and inevitably the myths woven by us, though they contain error, will also reflect a splintered fragment of the true light, the eternal truth that is with God. Indeed only by myth-making, only by becoming a 'sub-creator' and inventing stories, can Man ascribe to the state of perfection that he knew before the Fall.[5]

What this article seeks to show is that it is by endeavouring to actively learn from stories that people can move towards becoming more responsible and more religious.

Where Do We Go From Here?

Adapting Lonergan's method to teaching requires effort. It is not something to be followed as one would follow a recipe or a set of directions. Teachers need to be conscious of what occurs at each stage, and also of the goal of each activity. Recipes, prescriptions and other formulae 'may be repeated as often as you please, but the repetition yields no more than another instance of the original product.'[6] The method is not for those who simply want to duplicate experience. It is offered for use by anyone who wishes to learn from experience and move on to new levels of experience.

Lonergan's method can be used right across the curriculum, especially in relation to such issues as bullying, care for the earth, health and safety issues and the like which require commitment and courage on the part of pupils. The Social Personal and Health Education curriculum too 'fosters self-worth and self-confidence and places a particular emphasis on developing a sense of personal responsibility for one's own behaviour and actions'.[7] Lonergan's method has much to offer primary education.

Notes

1. C.S. Lewis, 'On Stories' Walter Hooper (ed.) *Of This and Other Worlds* (London: Fount Paperbacks, 1982), pp. 38-39.

2. R. Kearney, *On Stories* (London: Routledge, 2002), pp. 3-14.

3. P. O'Reilly and C. Maloney, *Alive-O 6, Teacher's Book*, (Dublin: Veritas, 2002), p. 23.

4. Kearney, *On Stories*, p. 4.

5. Walter Hooper (ed.) *Of This and Other Worlds*, preface, p. 15.

6. B. Lonergan, 'A Post-Hegelian Philosophy of Religion' in F.E. Crowe (ed.) *A Third Collection* (New York: Paulist Press, 1985), p. 204.

7. Department of Education and Science, *Primary School Curriculum: SPHE Teacher Guidelines*, (Dublin: DES, 1999), p. 3.

THE IMAGINATIVE, CARING AND HOPE-FILLED TEACHER

Rose Lynch

What we have loved others will love
And we will teach them how.
William Wordsworth

The future belongs to those who give the next generation reason to hope.
Teilhard de Chardin

Being a teacher is shaped, in the contemporary world, by the rapidly changing face of society. Cultural paradigms are collapsing and the worldview that served so well for centuries, in bringing not only progress and prosperity, but also a spirituality to support them, has reached the limits of its own possibilities. For educators, as social analysts J. Holland and P. Henriot suggest, generally today 'our response will be different, precisely because our context is different.'[1]

This changing face of society is reflected positively in the intense interest to live a fuller, deeper, more personal human life. Sandra Schneiders speaks of people striving for an integrated life. She experiences this not just in terms of self-integration and self-development but also in terms of self-transcendence, moving beyond self towards the horizon of ultimate concern, observing that

> there exists a hunger, a profound and authentic desire of 20th-21st-century humanity for wholeness in the midst of fragmentation, for community in the face of isolation and loneliness, for liberating transcendence, for meaning in life, for values that endure.[2]

Connected to the 'Wholeness of Life'

The *Primary School Curriculum*, 1999,[3] (*PSC*), outlines a holistic approach to the education of the child. It speaks of developing the effective, aesthetic, spiritual, and moral dimension of the child's experience. The teacher and the school support parents in progressing these significant areas of growth for children. However, interaction and engagement with primary school children also affects teachers and opens up their own spirituality to creative, caring and hope-filled possibilities. The word spirituality is a relatively new concept in education. It suggests, 'something vital and non-negotiable, lying at the heart of our lives. Spirituality is more than going to church. It is a way we express a living faith in a real world.'[4] The following comments are helpful in coming to understand what is meant by this term:

> By spiritual I mean the diverse ways we answer the heart's longing to be connected with the largeness of life – a longing that animates love and work, especially the work called teaching.[5]

> Spirituality cannot be limited to one part of an individual's reality, affecting them only in that dimension.

Nor is it something extra above and beyond their ordinary selves.[6]

Spirituality is not something added to our humanity. It is the very essence of what it means to be human.[7]

PSC speaks of the teacher's complex role as a caring facilitator and guide who leads children to the fullness of life, who interprets the children's learning needs and responds to them. The function of education is no longer merely a pragmatic one. It is a quest open to the spiritual dimension, setting out to develop the whole person. One of the challenges for educators today is to achieve the transition from the more traditional methods of teaching to a radically holistic approach. In responding to their pupils' individual needs teachers assist them on their journey to wholeness. The emphasis is shifted from curriculum content to the process of education, something that is at least as important. Through the graced journey of learning, teachers can instill an understanding of life as something meaningful and worthwhile. They can teach with a bias towards meaning and purpose. They can inspire learners to see 'the more in the midst'[8] of life and alert them to its mystery, stirring up in the process awe and reverence. As Sophie Freud says:

> We shouldn't ask what does a person need to know or to be able to do in order to fit into the existing social order. Instead we should ask what lives in each human being and what can be developed in him or her.[9]

Teacher and Learners Together
Successful teaching never happens by itself. Teachers influence the inner life of students. This requires a pattern of persistent

engagement and effort with the child at the centre. Teachers seek to create an atmosphere of hospitality in the classroom – a warm environment of welcome and acceptance where children can feel valued and have a sense that their uniqueness and potential are recognised. This can enable them to develop as people who have respect for themselves, for others and for the world in which they live. Parker Palmer, writing on the spirituality of education, speaks about hospitality as 'an atmosphere where everyone is accepted, where one can expose ignorance, express feelings, try out new hypotheses, challenge other ideas and engage in mutual criticism.'[10] Teachers, while always maintaining their responsibility as teachers, act also as companions to their students, nourishing the heart, mind, soul and body of those with whom they work. They engage deeply with the everyday experience of the students. In this way teachers are continually invited, as a consequence of their day-to-day work, to develop at so many levels, personally, relationally and spiritually.

This article, by considering themes arising directly out of the professional relationship of teachers with their students, offers an insight into the possibility of teachers developing their own spirituality out of who they are as teachers. By being aware of and engaging with certain themes that emerge within their day-to-day experience, teachers nurture both their students and themselves. Such themes would include:

- Encouraging imaginative interaction
- Developing a personal style of teaching
- Touching into the Transcendent
- Caring for students
- Facing self.

Encouraging Imaginative Interaction

Albert Einstein was of the opinion that imagination is far more important than knowledge. Educators are in a privileged position to stimulate the imagination of children. Imagination enables the learner to see 'the more in the midst' of the ordinary, to perceive what ought to be and have motivation to act accordingly. Imagination awakens and discloses the ordinarily unseen, the unheard of, and the unexpected. Teachers ask questions that activate the imagination, propose assignments that require creativity and applaud inventive efforts. Art, for example, is integral to teaching for deeper knowledge. Artwork greatly stimulates the imagination so that pupils can grow to appreciate not only art itself but also to develop the artist-within-themselves. The pleasure of creating can be a profound aesthetic experience even if what children produce is less than masterful. It can involve them with the meaning of human existence in a manner that mere description cannot achieve and offer possibilities for self-confrontation and self-identification. These experiences can open up new perspectives on what it is to learn and what it is to see.

Occasions can also be provided for students to be enriched by the art of others such as a trip to a gallery, a visit to art exhibitions or to see the work of local artists. Painting, poetry, music, sculpture and dance all engage by inviting the person to wonder, question and experience a wide range of meanings. Encounters with works of art elicit shock, adventure, exploration and wonder. Artistic processes such as storytelling, drama and movement also enhance the aesthetic education of students. In fact, Friedrich Froebel's theory of education[11] suggests that play is the highest phase of children's development, revealing the hidden inner natural life of humankind. Creative expression brings with it joy, freedom, inner contentment and peace with the world. As Emily Dickinson puts it:

'The Possible's slow fuse is lit by the imagination.'[12]

Developing a Personal Style of Teaching

The frontiers of teaching are infinitely broad and expanding. They continuously place demands on the teacher. The personal style that a teacher develops, such as being honest with students and with self, contributes enormously to the learning that takes place for both through the act of teaching. Teaching is focused on the transformation of outlook, on clearing up clouded horizons and on recognition of relationships. The way teachers handle complicated questions or difficulties, the way they speak about the material they are presenting, and the way they move from task to task, suggests something about how they perceive themselves. In facing the unfamiliar and the multiple vulnerability of each day teachers must decide how to communicate information, when to permit free, creative activity in place of following set requirements and when to nurture sensitivity. So much of what they do is precarious. Even in the best of circumstances they are faced with predicaments such as establishing control, motivating students and ensuring that learning occurs. In all of this activity their style of teaching influences everything.

The space for knowing and learning which they create in the classroom is a case in point. How teachers organise and present information and the attitude they have towards the responses of students affects the quality of the learning space. It is certainly more effective and gratifying to learn in an environment where the teacher not only speaks but also listens, not only proffers information but also poses questions while all the time welcoming the comments and insights of the students by encouraging them to think for themselves. A style of teaching which is open to receiving students' questions, comments and insights in turn invites them to become comfortable in offering their own thoughts. Such positive learning space is a powerful tool in imparting not only information but in inculcating attitudes such as openness, respect and caring. Such teaching requires humility, flexibility and adaptability on the part of the teacher.

Making space pertains, also, to the physical space of the classroom. Keeping the classroom free from clutter, for instance, conveys a sense of comfort and allows students to move about with ease. Desirable social behaviours such as respect for each other, adoption of an appropriate tone of voice, and the ability to listen to the opinions of others, are learned and practiced within the physical boundaries of the classroom. Personal boundaries are also established. Such boundaries help to define the learning space. They define the classroom as a focused and privileged place of learning. Boundaries help teachers to show students which actions are acceptable and which are not. Teachers also need personal courage to make reasonable and appropriate demands of students. They need a sense of their own authority. It is within the exercise of this authority that students find and retain their own freedom. When authority is genuine, obedience is freely given. Teachers, to be effective, must have the capacity to engender trust in the authority they have established with their students. This too requires a style of educating which is sure, honest and dynamic.

Touching the Transcendent

Palmer says that, 'spirituality, the human quest for connectedness, is not something that needs to be brought into or added to the curriculum, but is always present in education. It is at the heart of every subject we teach – where it waits to be brought forth.'[13] Educators can identify appropriate aesthetic and spiritual experiences embedded in the curriculum which provide a sense of the wonder of existence, evoking in students their own longing to give thanks for the gift of life. Painting, poetry, music, sculpture and dance engage by calling on the participants and practitioners to feel the presence of a wide range of meanings. John Dewey was adamant that nothing is learned from experience unless we 'interpret its meaning, ask the why and the wherefore of it, the reason behind it, and the consequences of it.'[14] Critical reflection is essential in any learning situation. It means pulling back the curtains to enable pupils to see better for themselves. Children can begin to reflect from an early age. A full education encourages children to think things through. Enabling children to reflect critically encourages a spiritual outlook on life, drawing them beyond themselves to find 'the more in the midst'. Encouraging children to listen to music, to take pleasure in the work of others, to look at paintings, and to listen to poetry can lead them to an inner experience where they sense and catch a glimmer of truth. Educators, together with parents, contribute to the liberation of children. They help them develop a personal identity and grow into wholeness. This allows them time and space to conceive the spiritual realities of life and to draw close to the transcendent, which is the source of ultimate meaning. Religious educator, Tom Groome, speaking about the aims of Catholic education highlights its all-embracing relational nature:

> When Catholic education enables people to have a life as well as make a living, when it gives them a sense of worthwhile purpose, when it enables them to make

meaning out of life, to choose and maintain their priorities, when it nurtures them in respect, reverence and responsibility as well as teaching the other 'four Rs', when it encourages people to grow in 'right relationships' with God, self, others and creation, when it fosters the full development of their talents and gifts, when it nurtures them in values and virtues that are life-giving for self and others – in sum, when it educates for life for all – then it is truly 'saving souls'. And such education must engage the souls of both teachers and students.[15]

Spirituality while central to the religion class is, of course, not confined to it. It can be encountered, for example, in maths and science class also. The notion of infinity, for instance, presents a great challenge for the human mind. Science topics can be taught in a way that points towards 'the more in the midst', encouraging learners to see for themselves the mystery, beauty, and wonder of the world. Encounters such as these can produce graced moments, blessed experiences, which call students into further wholeness. Witnessing such moments of enlightened growth is one of the greatest pleasures of teaching.

> At times our hands touch the presence of an active force
> that is not ours,
> and it is precisely because it is not our own
> that it fills us with wonder and deep joy.[16]

Caring for Students
The commitment to caring for the well being of students is at the centre of a teacher's spirituality. Students bring a host of personal concerns to the classroom, as do teachers. Yet, it is

teachers who must put to one side their own needs, moods, anxieties and concerns. Their obligation is to teach, which is a form of service to others. Qualities such as compassion, integrity, dedication, empathy, truthfulness, attentiveness and love are essential qualities in any educator. The moral obligation involved makes teaching a most demanding task. It is not surprising, then, that everyone will fall short, occasionally, of his or her own expectations. Young people are more likely to be affected by teachers who themselves are questioning, pondering and learning. Teachers, by caring for their students, encourage them to learn how to make decisions of principle for themselves, and how to reflect, to articulate, and to act in good faith.

Teachers are also called upon to be sources of moral counsel. They must routinely put their own integrity and sense of judgment on public display. Teaching is always both an intellectual and a moral endeavor. A teacher cannot simply preach an ethic of caring. She or he must live it: 'Everything we do as teachers has moral implications. Through dialogue, modeling practice and the assignment of best motive, a caring teacher nurtures the ethical ideal.'[17]

Teachers must endeavour to help students become acquainted with their moral heritage in religion and literature. Teachers should feel able, for example, to declare that there is such a thing as moral knowledge and that religious tradition has something valuable to say about it. Basic decency, human rights, and vice and virtue, have been reflected on over several thousands of years of civilization. This knowledge is preserved in the religious inheritance that has come down to this day by means of factors such as the teachings, traditions and lives of the people with whom a common story is shared. Throughout history, moral education has been accomplished using moral tales and parables which propose and embody admirable ethical behaviour. Genuine care for students, then, will happily support behaviour codes that emphasise civility, kindness and honesty.

Facing Self

Teachers, just like everyone else, have to face the multiple vulnerabilities of each day. If they want to grow as authentic people, they must learn to talk to friends and to one another about their inner lives – about their identity and integrity. The more they engage with students as people, the more they affirm their own incompleteness. They become more aware of the spaces still to be explored, desires still to be uncovered, and possibilities still to be opened. For many of them a sense of incompleteness is heightened by how they handle their time and their own vulnerability. Many feel there is never enough time to do what needs to be done. They are faced with establishing priorities for themselves in respect of personal needs, family concerns, the demands of friendship and professional tasks. Teachers grow weary of performing, entertaining and filling up the emptiness of others. They tire of trying to stimulate, encourage, comfort, and discipline students. If they open their hearts to the wisdom of experience, it is less burdensome. In doing their own inner work and building up their relationships they can explore their deepest and most sacred places, coming to an understanding of who they are becoming. This requires being continually awake and open to various levels of their own life and intentionally nurturing themselves as they would their students. Every now and then, they look upon themselves with self-awareness and notice something new. These are the moments when there is a chance to change and to flourish. These are moments of profound paradox:

The paradoxes of my life are related to being a student and teacher of topics that intimately touch my own and other people's lives. Such a field demands total devotion to its subject matter, as well as providing rich and varied life experiences. It demands tight self-discipline and loose creativity. It demands openness to people and absorption with ideas, protection of time and energy, as well as endless commitment to students. It demands both solitude and many human encounters. It demands skills of objectivity, observation and involvement, distance as well as intimacy. It demands self-assurance, power and humility.[18]

Solitude and Silence

Teachers need solitude and silence in order to find the power and the courage to maximise the work they aspire to do. Such time is not a luxury. It is a necessity. Surrounded by noise and distraction, teachers too can lose their connection with the source of their being. Precisely because they give so much of themselves, some desert time is crucial. Moments of solitude have a way of restoring perspective and renewing depth. Silence can bring back openness to the wonders of life. The uniqueness of the individual is re-established. Peace and calm are re-instated. Divine wisdom waits in such stillness and silence. A period of time each day, or at least each week, worked into a schedule and faithfully adhered to, is a wellspring from which life is refreshed. Sr Stanislaus Kennedy refers us to the wisdom of Thomas Merton's insight:

Let there be a place somewhere in which you can breathe naturally, quietly, and not have to take your breath in continuous short gasps. A place where your mind can be idle and forget its concerns, descend into silence, and reflect and worship in secret.[19]

Balance in Life

Balance in life is essential. A sense of order, awe, proportion and perspective, giving each part of life honour and recognition, is life giving. As with all people, teachers gradually understand that they are called to live a rhythm of life that includes the natural, the spiritual, the social, the productive, the physical, and the personal. They need more than work and adequate remuneration – things such as play, friendship, spiritual growth, intellectual stimulation and harmony with nature. Finding ways of establishing some distance from their everyday concerns and from their work is essential for a healthy balanced lifestyle.

Awareness of Time

Daily life is ruled by schedules but there is a need for a keen awareness of the time one possesses. Educators need to develop a sense of ownership of the world and of the times they live in. They need to have a vision of where they are going. Everyday is gift for the fulfillment of the purposes they have recognised in their lives. With a sense of purpose people don't just drift. They listen to their call and discern what is right for them and for their community at any particular time.

Renewing the Self

It is imperative that teachers embrace reflection, self-renewal and personal development. As well as satisfying their own inner self, this commitment will generate greater presence to and enthusiasm for their work. Educators, by the work they do, are kept fresh, alive and open to new possibilities all the time. Creativity in their professional lives has the potential to affect them personally.

Conclusion

In conclusion there is need to keep exploring and to keep alive that sense of adventure which is an essential component of the work of teaching. An imaginative, caring and hope-filled heart serves teachers well in their work with children. This work, it may be expected, influences the whole of their lives, inspiring them to become imaginative, caring people full of hope for themselves, for others, for their community and for the world at large:

> Our deepest fear is not that we are inadequate
> Our deepest fear is that we are powerful
> beyond measure,
> It is not in some of us, it is in everyone.
> *Nelson Mandela*

> When you start your journey to Ithaca then pray
> that the road is long,
> full of adventure, full of knowledge.
> *Constantine Cavafy*

Notes

1. J. Holland and P. Henriot, *Social Analysis: Linking Faith and Justice* (New York: Orbis Books, 1995), p. 67.
2. S. Schneiders, 'Spirituality in the Academy' *Theological Studies* 50/2(1989), pp. 676-697.
3. Department of Education and Science, *Primary School Curriculum: Introduction* (The Stationary Office, 1999), p. 27.
4. J. Chittister, *Wisdom Distilled from the Daily.* (San Francisco: Harper & Row, 1990), pp. 4-5.
5. P. Palmer, *The Courage to Teach* (San Francisco: Jossey-Bass, 1998), p. 5.
6. G. Byrne, 'Embracing Life at Its Fullest: Spirituality for Religious Educators and School Chaplains' J. Norman (ed.) *At the Heart of*

Education: School Chaplaincy and Pastoral Care (Dublin: Veritas, 2004), p. 185.

7. K. Treston, *Paths and Stories: Spirituality for Teachers and Catechists* (Dublin: Veritas, 1991), p. 10.

8. T.H. Groome, *Educating for Life: A Spiritual Vision for Every Teacher and Parent* (Allen, Texas: Thomas More, 1998), p. 132.

9. S. Freud, 'The Passion and Challenge of Teaching' M. Okazawa, R.J. Anderson, R. Traver (eds.) *Teachers, Teaching and Teacher Education* (Cambridge, Mass: Harvard University Press, 1987), p. 130.

10. P. Palmer, *To Know as We Are Known: A Spirituality of Education* (San Francisco: Harper & Row, 1983), pp. 71-74.

11. For more on Friedrich Froebal (1782-1852), see Carmel Scanlon's chapter in this publication.

12. E. Dickinson, 'The Gleam of an Heroic Act' from *Complete Poems of Emily Dickinson* (1955).

13. P. Palmer, 'Evoking the Spirit in Public Education', *Educational Leadership* 56/4(1999), p. 8.

14. J. Dewey, 'My Pedagogic Creed', M.S. Dworkin (ed.) *Dewey in Education*, Classics in Education 3 (New York: Teacher's College, Columbia University, 1971), p. 32.

15. T.H. Groome, 'Forging in the Smithy of the Teacher's Soul', N. Prendergast and L. Monahan (eds.) *Reimagining the Catholic School* (Dublin: Veritas, 2003), p. 40.

16. S. Cavalletti, *The Religious Potential of the Child* (Chicago: Liturgy Training Publications, 1992), p. 52.

17. N. Nodding, *Caring: A Feminine Approach to Ethics and Moral Education* (Berkley: University of California Press, 1984), p. 179.

18. S. Freud, 'The Passion and Challenge of Teaching', p. 134.

19. Cited in S. Kennedy, *Gardening the Soul* (London: Simon and Schuster, 2001).

HOME, PARISH AND SCHOOL IN PARTNERSHIP

CONFIRMATION

Sacrament of Initiation, Commitment or Departure?

Neasa Ní Argadáin

At the INTO Special Conference on Religious Education, convened in Mullingar in November 2002, a suggestion that Confirmation be postponed until post-primary school was enthusiastically greeted with rousing applause by the audience.[1] Clearly the delegates believed that this would solve the ever increasing problem of teacher frustration, or 'Confirmation fatigue'.

After working for five years as a diocesan adviser in Dublin, I noticed that primary school teachers are generally well-disposed towards teaching religion. While my experience is anecdotal, it is confirmed by recent research of the INTO, the Marino Institute of Education and by the Veritas commissioned report, *Islands Apart*, which indicated that teachers remain by and large positively disposed towards the teaching of religion.[2] They enjoy it and so do their pupils. Their one major area of concern or stress is sacramental preparation, particularly Confirmation. Teachers often feel isolated in their role as religious educators. Many of the children in their classrooms have no faith background at home and parents tend to delegate religious education to the school. Teachers also feel increasingly distanced from parish life as the shortage of priests and their reluctance to visit schools makes an impact. Hence the title of the Veritas report: the three islands of home, school and parish are drifting further apart.

Another concern felt keenly by teachers of sixth class is that many children preparing for Confirmation may not have been to church regularly since their first Communion. Teachers are becoming increasingly frustrated that the Church and the sacraments, which many of them cherish, are being somehow devalued by the process of near-automatic sacramental preparation. They feel very strongly that Confirmation has become a rite of passage out of primary school and out of the Church. Is the solution, then, to move Confirmation to post-primary or should we reflect first on how we arrived at this point? Something of the confusion and frustration of teachers may be gathered from the following:

> For the average person, sacraments are like crushed roses in an old book. We admire them, but really we don't know who put them there, why they are at this particular page, what significance it all has … and a host of other background questions.[3]

Teachers, as pragmatists, want something done to rectify the situation, sooner rather than later. In conversations with teachers they usually offer two solutions to the Confirmation dilemma. One is to transfer much of sacramental preparation to the parish setting. The other is to postpone Confirmation until a later age, preferably around transition year in post-primary school. While both of these suggestions contain some merit, it is debatable whether either or both might provide a solution, although each may go some way towards resolving the immediate difficulties of teachers. Moving sacramental preparation into the parish would undoubtedly address the 'automatic reception' notion and would demand a greater level of commitment to attend Sunday school or its equivalent. But who would take on this task? How and when would catechists be trained? Would they be paid or would they be volunteers?

Teachers, being resourceful people, accept the situation in which they find themselves and they try to make the best of it. They get on with the task in hand. Consequently, they accept the notion of Confirmation as it is presented in the sixth-class textbooks, namely as a sacrament of maturity and mission, a personal appropriation of the promises made on one's behalf at Baptism. With such an image, it is easy to see how postponing the sacrament until mid-teens might be more appealing. However, this would be like admiring the crushed roses mentioned above without questioning where they come from. It is like looking at the immediate difficulty through too narrow a lens and failing to see the big picture. Strategic rather than tactical questions need to be asked. One needs to look beyond the immediate manifestation of the Confirmation dilemma and question the fundamental assumptions about the sacrament. Only then can one discern what is worth retaining and what needs to be altered. This in turn will facilitate planning for real and effective change and renewal, restoring the sacrament of Confirmation to its rightful place of honour in the life of the faith community.

A History of Confirmation as a Sacrament

Reflection should begin by considering the origin and development of Confirmation. Of all the sacraments, it has possibly the most contentious history and is often referred to as 'the problem of Confirmation' in the literature. Its chequered past has led to the emergence of a bewildering variety of theologies. One tends to think of Confirmation in terms only of that with which one is familiar such as a ceremony in sixth class, which involves huge preparation, wearing new clothes and collecting lots of money. Pausing to consider that it may be different in other places or at other times rarely occurs.

The Early Church

Many consider the Pentecost story, as described in Acts 2, to be the foundational event for an understanding of Confirmation. The disciples were 'all together in one place ... all of them were filled with the Holy Spirit and began to speak in other languages.' (Acts 2: 1-4). There is certainly no record in the gospels that Christ specifically confirmed anyone in the way now recognised as Confirmation. Historical investigation reveals that the rite of Confirmation varied in different places and at different times.

In the early Church, the rite of Confirmation was integrated into the initiation ritual as a post-baptismal blessing or dismissal by the bishop. As the Church grew in numbers the initiation rite evolved into Baptism, followed by a blessing from the bishop at a later time. The latter blessing eventually evolved into the sacrament of Confirmation. In the Eastern Church, however, the initiation ceremony has remained as one rite down to the present day. This practice gives rise to 'The Patristic Model', as noted by Mark Searle,[4] which envisages Confirmation being restored to its original place as part of the total Christian initiation ceremony, thus retrieving the ancient practice of the Church.

A View From the Middle Ages

Sacraments began when people tried to re-tell, re-enact and re-live their foundational stories in symbol and ritual. 'Doctrine takes time to develop. We first tell our lived experiences in story and celebrate them in festivity. Logical analysis and systematic concepts come later, after further reflection.'⁵

In time, people began to focus on the ritual rather than on the earlier stories or meanings. The theologians of the fifth and sixth centuries attempted to articulate the meaning of the rites as they were celebrated in their time and place. They had little knowledge of what led to those particular practices. After the separation of Baptism and Confirmation into two distinct rites it was natural that theologians would try to provide explanations which took this separation for granted and so a theology of two gifts developed. Confirmation lost much of its initiation character and became known as a 'strengthening' of Baptism.

During the Dark Ages (600-1000 AD) there was little time or demand in Europe for theological reflection or study. This was a difficult time for the Church. It wasn't until the thirteenth century, when Europe regained a sense of calm and peace and the early medieval universities were founded, that study of subjects such as liturgy recommenced.

The complex task of looking for explanations amid conflicting sources was undertaken, but in the meantime, much of the earlier wisdom had been lost. The rituals became standardised and therefore confined. The rituals were becoming more bound to theology and doctrine than to experience. By 1274 at the Council of Lyons, the Church was ready to declare that there were seven sacraments, a number that signified wholeness. Confirmation was officially a separate sacrament, a conclusion that was re-iterated by the Council of Florence in 1439. Thomas Aquinas (1225-1274), recognised as the most comprehensive and influential of the medieval theologians took for granted that Confirmation was and always had been, a separate sacrament. He proposed that correctly performed sacraments were valid.

Unfortunately, this led to minimalist liturgies, where the bare essentials became the norm. In an age when few people were literate and when liturgy was the primary source of catechesis, this was a huge loss. Confirmation, at this time, conformed to what could be described as 'The Roman Model', which considered it to be an independent sacrament separate from Baptism. This understanding saw Confirmation as necessary to confer the Holy Spirit. Remnants of this approach remain in our present model. One need only recall here the words of the bishop, 'Be sealed with the gift of the Holy Spirit', to appreciate this. Despite being gifted with the Holy Spirit at Baptism, a further ratification by a more senior minister, namely a bishop, is apparently deemed necessary.

Reformation Influences

Another important development was the rejection by Protestant reformers of the doctrine of seven sacraments and their retention only of Baptism and Eucharist as sacraments. From the sixteenth century they opted for a model in which Confirmation was considered an affirmation of faith. Many Lutheran and Calvinist Churches retain this model today, as an almost coming of age ceremony, a celebration of mature faith. Surprisingly, perhaps, the ideology of this 'Reformation Model' is widespread in the Catholic Church. In Ireland today it is frequently proposed as an alternative to our present situation. The thinking behind this model focuses on maturity and commitment, neither of which necessarily are essential to initiation, the original function of Confirmation.

Twentieth-Century Developments

Towards the end of the nineteenth century, the practice arose in France of receiving the Eucharist prior to Confirmation, a practice later encouraged by Pope Pius X. This was highly significant as it reversed the traditional order of the sacraments. Baptism, first Eucharist (with first Penance beforehand) and then Confirmation became the habitual custom.

Throughout the twentieth century, historical research and theological reflection recovered many of the early sources of sacramental practice and revealed the deficiencies in much of our understanding of sacramental theology. This willingness to seek and learn led to the Second Vatican Council convened by Pope John XXIII in 1962. Vatican II sought to reform Christian initiation, not in order to introduce novelty or meaningless change, but out of respect for what had been discovered through ongoing historical and liturgical research.

IN SEARCH OF A CONTEMPORARY THEOLOGY OF CONFIRMATION

As already noted, practice of Confirmation varied greatly at different times depending on circumstances. What may not have been expected is that the practice and celebration of Confirmation today should vary so dramatically from country to country and even from diocese to diocese. It seems astonishing that in one universal Church different sacramental methods and systems apply, depending on location, interpretation of the sources and theology. Confirmation is frequently described as 'a sacrament in search of a theology.'[6] It may be more correct to say: 'There are several forms of Confirmation, each in search of a theology.'[7]

With regard to Confirmation today, two main models are frequently cited. The language used varies depending on the author but basically opinion falls into either the Pastoral-Catechetical Model or the Liturgical-Celebration Model.

The Pastoral-Catechetical Model

This model is frequently associated with coming of age, celebrating Christian maturity, a rite of passage into Christian adulthood. The present experience in Ireland contains much of this model. While we confirm at twelve, an age still considered to be pre-adolescent, we highlight many of the themes associated with maturity and witness in our cathechetical programmes. Much emphasis is put on the element of personal commitment; that which parents accepted on one's behalf in Baptism, now becomes the young Christian's responsibility. This idea is not without merit. At twelve years of age there is a sense of otherness, when young people are beginning to take on new responsibilities and such a ritual, as Confirmation, seems to relate and respond to that.

The notion of postponing Confirmation until late adolescence is popular with many writers who favour the pastoral-cathechetical model. It is also gaining favour among many primary teachers in Ireland on whom, as has already been mentioned, the burden of sacramental preparation often falls. Many teachers consider their sixth-class pupils too immature to see beyond the social trimmings of Confirmation to the significance of the encounter.

There is a certain coherence between the sacraments and the natural cycles of life into which adolescent Confirmation slots, anthropologically if not liturgically. Ideally this should entail a process that candidates could opt into rather than fall into as the near-automatic reception of Confirmation that prevails facilitates. As teenagers, the *confirmandi* are likely to be more aware of the implication of witness and mission than would be the case with younger children. It would involve a commitment on their part to prepare for Confirmation, not just as individuals, but also as members of their own families and the wider parish. They would become more visible within the parish community, perhaps finding their own place and voice there. Such a model would inevitably mean that many would not 'opt in'. While this may cause concern, it is hardly any more damaging than confirming the multitudes simply out of habit. Indeed, smaller numbers would allow for greater flexibility in the way in which the ceremony itself is celebrated, re-establishing it perhaps, as part of the Easter Vigil or allowing it become the focus of the Pentecost liturgy.

However, writers such as Paul Turner are highly critical of this model. He is dismissive of social and pastoral reasons for adolescent Confirmation, claiming it is an attempt to surmount the conflict between adolescents and their parents and teachers.[8]

The Liturgical-Celebration Model

Many influential commentators such as Aidan Kavanagh and Mark Searle reject the pastoral-catechetical model as being too far removed from Confirmation's origin as a rite of initiation and are anxious to see the sacrament restored to its original context. In practice, this also includes reinstating the traditional sequence of the sacraments of Baptism, Confirmation and Eucharist as celebrated in the Eastern Church. In Ireland, this would entail celebrating Confirmation prior to or in conjunction with first Communion.

This may sound curious to people who believe that our present candidates are too young and immature to realise the significance of the commitment they are undertaking. But this is the crux of the matter. Those who support a liturgical-celebration model do not consider Confirmation to be a sacrament of commitment or maturity. Instead they emphasise its initiatory roots.

This model is already being piloted in some parishes in the diocese of Sacramento in California where Confirmation and first Eucharist are celebrated at the same ceremony. The dioceses of Glasgow and Salford have also piloted a format where children are confirmed about a year before their first Communion (which remains at age seven or eight). In such a model, Confirmation is seen as a celebration of the gift of the Holy Spirit rather than an acknowledgement of spiritual or other maturity. The children do not have to prove themselves worthy of the gift of Confirmation by attending and completing a rigorous catechetical syllabus.

A consequence of celebrating Confirmation prior to first Communion is that it would restore Eucharist to its proper place as source and summit of the sacramental life. There may be a sense at present that Confirmation is a higher-ranking sacrament then Eucharist; after all, it cannot be received until one is 'mature', it can only be celebrated once and a bishop usually officiates. False signals may unwittingly be sent about the order of the sacraments suggesting that initiation is completed by Confirmation rather than by receiving the Eucharist.

Those who see Confirmation as a passing-out parade may be concerned that in this model those who now leave the Church at twelve would instead leave at seven, directly after first Communion. They may be correct. But perhaps the mistake lies in confirming twelve-year-olds at present who have no desire to be initiated fully into the Church and are unmoved by concepts such as commitment, witness or mission. Is it appropriate to maintain this practice, as a way of keeping people formally involved for a little longer?

Points to Ponder

Clearly, the sacrament of Confirmation can be celebrated at different times and in different ways depending on one's understanding of theology. It may be opportune to consider a new model of Confirmation for our time. Five essential points emerge as crucial to finding an appropriate celebration of the sacrament of Confirmation in Ireland today.

A New Vision

There was no reform of the seven sacraments in the Roman Catholic tradition from the Roman Missal of 1570 until Vatican II. Sacraments were seen as duties rather than as personal encounters between the human and the Divine. It is now possible to think of sacraments in a way that is different from Aquinas and the scholastic theologians. Sacraments may be understood as encounters that are as relevant and meaning-filled for Christians today as they were for the early Christian Community of first-century Palestine. This may be particularly difficult in relation to Confirmation, not least because in Ireland its image is so tied to school and to pre-adolescence. It is often considered less appealing and attractive than other sacraments.

To contemplate a new image for Confirmation is not to judge the previous images deficient. Nor is it to consider change for change sake. Instead it is to regard Confirmation as a spiritual encounter and to correct the perception that it is a ritual of completion or maturity, a rite of passage out of primary school and sometimes out of Church. The task of theologians is not just to recover the past, but also to redefine its significance for today. This will be an ongoing process involving adaptation to cultural and practical changes as they arise, so that the Gospel may always ring true.

Various people have come up with different, sometimes controversial images for the future of Confirmation. Kavanagh is vehemently opposed to Confirmation as it is celebrated presently, for example in the Irish experience, where the preparation focuses on the mature confirming of the gifts received at Baptism[9] and where the celebration is more appropriate to a rite of passage out of primary school. He sees the value of having a liturgical ceremony which acknowledges adolescence as a rite of passage, but feels that we could develop other more appropriate rituals, especially in the area of reconciliation, thus reflecting in a prayerful, liturgical way that which is happening in the lives of the community. Bernard Cooke also suggests this process as an appropriate way of nourishing people towards authentic faith.[10] Michael Drumm and Tom Gunning outline ten different models of Christian initiation[11] some of which envisage Confirmation being revisited at various stages.

For ecumenical reasons, many theologians and liturgists would like to see a restoration of the ancient and traditional process of initiation as has been maintained in the Eastern Church. Current Confirmation practice in the Roman Church bears little relation to the Eastern practice of chrismation. In fact, the Roman Catholic position and that of many of the reformed Churches is, in practice, quite close. Despite their rejection of the sacrament of Confirmation as having no scriptural basis, many in the reformed tradition maintain a similar rite for its spiritual and pastoral value. The Lutheran Churches recognise 'a Confirmation ceremony' as a commemoration of Baptism where the connection with catechesis is most prominent.[12] Anglicans also celebrate a Confirmation rite as a conclusion to catechesis, while the Reformed-Calvinist Churches celebrate the completion of catechesis with admission to the Lord's Supper. Which, if any, of these could contribute to an appropriate vision?

God's Grace at Work in Us

Sacraments were often defined as signs instituted by Christ to bestow grace. Does this imply that grace is absent without sacraments, or that grace can only be conferred in a sacramental context: 'Too often we have spoken of the Lord's presence in the sacraments as though He were absent elsewhere.'[13] I am reminded of a story of a friend who often gives a lift in her car to some elderly sisters. They insist on reciting a prayer 'to keep them safe' before their journey begins. This amuses my friend who remarked: 'Do they think that God won't be in the car with them if they don't say the prayer?' We often do this sort of thing, imagining that we can control God by our actions. God works by God's own will, not by that of humans. Grace is God-given; it is God's initiative. How we recognise or react to that grace depends on our receptivity and our response. Nonetheless, this does not alter the fundamental truth that grace is God's gift, freely given and untethered by any doctrinal or historical precedents.

One does not wish to suggest that grace is not given in sacraments, but merely to expand our vision of grace, to see God's gift in many of life's daily encounters, both within and beyond the sacraments. God is not made present in the sacraments. God is already and always present. The sacraments are opportunities for Christians to heighten their awareness of that presence, to acknowledge and celebrate it and to respond to it in an appropriate way. The Apostles and early Christians didn't attend church to find God. They believed that God's grace, God's gift, was Christ present among them. They acknowledged that gift of presence in ritual ways, which were later recognised as sacraments.

The reality that God is always with us can often be missed. God's grace is always available. In what way does this influence thinking on Confirmation? It upholds the belief that Confirmation is a gift of God, rather than a personal commitment. It is God's work, not ours. It is an occasion to acknowledge and celebrate and respond to the gift of God's Spirit, already present in the person since Baptism. Sacraments are not about commodities. They are about relationships, to be lived rather than received. Christian initiation is about making people aware of God's presence in their lives. It is about cultivating and supporting faith so that believers can come to see God 'in the bits and pieces of everyday.'[14]

Fully Conscious and Active Participation

More research and study on the meaning of the sacraments has been accomplished in the last fifty years than in the preceeding centuries. The Council of Trent effectively froze any subsequent development of the sacraments. Much wisdom has been uncovered and recovered by theologians and liturgists in recent years and the overall trend has been towards a more experiential understanding of the sacraments.

Edward Schillebeekx has much to teach us about considering sacraments as *encounters,* as events for participants, rather than for mere spectators. He highlights the sacraments as humanity's encounter with God in the person of Jesus Christ. Through the Incarnation, God became present in humanity and remains present there, in the ordinary occurrences of everyday life. We may search elsewhere for God, but God is already here, present and waiting to be discovered.

We know that sacraments are God's action, not ours, but we should ensure that nothing we do hampers or hinders the possibility of a real fruitful encounter between God and the assembled people. Teachers often feel that the way in which we celebrate Confirmation presently does little to facilitate such an encounter. Many share this concern.

Sacramental Process

Traditionally, sacraments tend to be seen as one-day events. If life is thought of as a grace-filled journey, then there is a need to consider the sacramental process as well as the sacramental moment. How does this affect one's understanding of Confirmation? Firstly, it will take the emphasis off 'the day' with all the attendant fuss over clothes, gifts, music and so on. In a Confirmation process, many significant milestones would be marked en route to the Confirmation itself. There might be an initial enrolment ceremony, a catechetical programme, a commitment to undertake specific duties, a missioning ceremony, a renewal of baptism promises etc. If focus is placed on process rather than on product, then there is need to reconsider whether Confirmation should automatically be in sixth class. Should it be automatic at all? Should the preparation for it remain school-based or should it be more closely connected to the parish community, as Orla Walsh suggests in her article in this publication focused on preparation for first Communion? Process implies follow-up as well as preparation, and schools are ill-positioned to follow up on students once they have left the school. If initiation is a process, can it be assumed that everyone reaches the stage of desiring Confirmation at the same age? If we think of process, then we must consider the notion of readiness, of preparedness. Perhaps not everyone will want to take this step on the journey. What part, if any, does personal, family or community faith play in furthering the process? Is our role to nourish faith to a stage of preparedness for Confirmation or is it to confirm the masses and hope that God's work will be fruitful in at least some of them.

Sacramental Celebration

In appealing for consideration of the sacraments in terms of process there is no suggestion of a belittling or a negating of the significance of the sacramental moment. 'Sacraments mark milestones and further the journey.'[15] Sacraments are those specific points in life when believers stop to acknowledge and celebrate the significance of the journey. We must be conscious of retaining a sense of the sacred in the process, that there are certain festive occasions when the community assembles to remember and renew their stories and to celebrate their meaning. God doesn't wait for sacraments in order to confer grace. Instead sacraments are celebrations of the grace already present in our lives. Confirmation is the celebration of the gift of the Holy Spirit already present in us, in the Church and in the world.

We must consider how people can be brought to a point of readiness for such full, conscious and active participation in the ceremony. We must look at how best we can facilitate an experiential and meaningful celebration of Confirmation for young people who have little or no affiliation to Church. If we are to be authentic then I think we need to accept people as they are. Christians believe that God is present, bidden or unbidden. People are graced whether or not they are regular churchgoers. Accepting people as they are is not synonymous with automatic reception of sacraments. It does not preclude challenging candidates so as to stretch their religious imagination either through catechesis or through some form of parish work or mission activity. But accepting candidates as they are implies that, as a community, they are helped to find God in their own experience, not in ours. We neither believe nor accept that God is absent in the culture of young people. We are just not always accustomed to seeking God there.

Conclusion

Clearly there is no easy solution to the Confirmation dilemma. The root of the problems encountered in Ireland in relation to automatic reception, school-based preparation and the 'rite of departure' stem from a lack of understanding of the origin, meaning and theology of the sacraments.

The first crucial decision facing us as a community of believers is whether we want to celebrate Confirmation as a sacrament of initiation or as a sacrament of maturity. Each requires a different context and different catechesis. In effect, at present, we are doing neither. As a sacrament of initiation serious consideration needs to be given to celebrating it prior to first Communion, thus restoring the traditional order of the sacraments of initiation and promoting Eucharist to its rightful place as source and summit of sacramental life. If, on the other hand, the image of Confirmation as a sacrament of maturity or commitment is chosen then it may be time to defer it until late adolescence when it can be more realistically presented as a personal profession of faith. Whichever path is favoured, there are lessons to be learned:

- Any change should be preceded by a process of consultation and evangelisation and/or catechesis with as wide a representation of the People of God as possible
- Any focus should be on the overall vision of Church and sacraments rather than becoming entangled in minor or local quandaries
- Any future sacramental preparation must site the groundwork in the family and parish rather than the school. While, in many

cases, the Catholic school is the only real 'parish' community a child can identify with, this is, in ways, a false support, which by its nature cannot be present throughout the child's life. It may be an effective part of parish, but it should not be the total experience.

In the end it must be remembered that Christ founded a community of believers. It is in the community that the Spirit resides, not in any doctrinal tomes. Many people have lost their connection to the institutional Church but they are still gifted with the Spirit. The image of Church as 'it' has been replaced, thankfully, by a realisation of the Church as 'us'. The Spirit is moving in us and through us, asking us continually to consider how we can best respond to God's grace.

Notes

1. See Irish National Teachers' Organisation, *Teaching Religion in the Primary School: Issues and Challenges* (Dublin: INTO Publications, 2004).
2. See M. Kennedy, *Islands Apart* (Dublin: Veritas, 2000).
3. W.J. Bausch, *A New Look at the Sacraments* (1977), reprinted (Cork: The Mercier Press, 1983), p. 10.
4. See M. Searle, *Christening: The Making of Christians* (Collegeville, MN: Liturgical Press, 1980).
5. T. Guzie, *The Book of Sacramental Basics* (New York: Paulist Press, 1981), p. 38.
6. W.J. Bausch, *A New Look at the Sacraments*, p. 94.
7. F. Quinn, 'Confirmation: Does it Make Sense', *Ecclesia Orans* (1988), p. 325.
8. See P. Turner, *The Baby in Solomon's Court* (New York: Paulist, 1993).
9. See A. Kavanagh, *Confirmation: Origins and Reform* (New York: Pueblo, 1988).
10. B. Cooke, *Sacraments and Sacramentality* (1983), reprinted (Mystic: Twenty-Third Publications, 1987), p. 147.
11. See M. Drumm and T. Gunning, *A Sacramental People,* Vol. 1 (Dublin: Columba, 1999), p. 44-75.
12. See L. Leijssen, 'Confirmation in Context', *Louvain Studies* 20(1995), p. 301.
13. T. Guzie, *The Book of Sacramental Basics*, p. 64.
14. P. Kavanagh (ed.) *Patrick Kavanagh: The Complete Poems* (Newbridge: Goldsmith Press, 1984), p. 79.
15. M. Searle, *Christening: The Making of Christians*, p. 183.

CELEBRATING COMMUNION WITH THE LORD AND WITH EACH OTHER

Parish-Based Sacramental Preparation

Orla Marie Walsh

One May morning as I dropped my eldest son off for school we noticed quite a busy gathering at the school gate. As we drew closer we saw that it was the first-class pupils chattering to each other. Having made their first Holy Communion on the previous Saturday the girls were beautiful in their pretty dresses and veils, some with tiaras and matching bags. The boys looked dapper in their jackets and pants. Shiny shoes replaced scuffed trainers. Shiny ringlets ousted plain plaits. As we walked closer to the wave of excited seven year olds I couldn't help but overhear the chatter. Sadly, the topic of conversation was about money, each child boasting about what they had gathered and how they were they going to spend it. These children had a wonderful teacher who had practised and prayed with each of them in preparation for their special day. Seemingly, however, they had nothing else to chat about, nothing else to wonder at. While one would not expect these children to be discussing 'the real presence', the absence of some sense of the rite of initiation they had just celebrated is a cause of some concern. This and other similar experiences seem to suggest that good sacramental preparation can only breathe new life into the Catholic community if it receives immediate and energetic attention by all concerned. This article, accordingly, focuses on the particular understanding and needs of the community as it prepares its young people to participate in the sacramental life of the Church.

INITIATION INTO THE PARISH COMMUNITY

Sacramental preparation ought to be a central concern of the community called Church and begin with the parish community. The establishment of teams to coordinate sacramental preparation is becoming a feature of sacramental life. In many instances a good beginning has been made in assisting parents and families prepare for the Baptism of their children. Such teams should also extend to the other sacraments of initiation facilitating children from the community who are preparing for the sacraments of Confirmation and Eucharist. The very word 'team' suggests a group of people who work together in a resourceful and dynamic fashion with a shared focus. At present, many pupils who are preparing for their first Confession, first Holy Communion and Confirmation do so in their local Catholic National School without a specialist teacher and with little community support. The existence of satisfactorily qualified and committed primary-school teachers does not address the need for the parish to be recognised as the community of faith, support and loving action within which these young people are invited to participate and belong. In the area of catechesis, the Church hands over much responsibility to teachers. As a result, the sense of belonging and participation in a local parish may not be fully realised or even understood by many young people.

Parish-based initiatives should therefore be encouraged. A programme facilitated by the parish would enable parents and children to work and learn together while being guided by a team comprising for instance, a catechist, a member of the local clergy, and other committed members of the parish community. This is not to suggest that the local school would no longer be involved in sacramental preparation: quite the opposite. School preparation for the sacraments would run in conjunction with a parish programme. School personnel, even if not living locally, would be invited to participate in the activities of the faith community to which the children belong. The joint programme would depend on partnership, where the opinion, experience and creativity of all would be appreciated. Everyone would strive towards a common goal with shared aims and objectives.

In a Spirit of Partnership
The preparation necessary for such a joint approach has in fact taken place progressively over the past three decades. A growing number of lay Catholics have undergone theological, pastoral and catechetical training to a high standard. Many parish communities have at their disposal lay members who might be invited, for example, to coordinate and educate the kind of parish-based sacramental preparation teams being considered here. In conjunction with parents these teams could create the atmosphere of cooperation between parish and school suggested above. Local adult religious education initiatives, parish *Faith Friends* programmes for the young people, and Family Mass celebrations of enrolment for the sacraments at which parishioners are present, could be very supportive of a partnership approach. Catechists and chaplains trained for post-primary schools might also, for instance, be interested in making themselves available for parish sacramental programmes. Some parishes or clusters of parishes might even be in a position to appoint a full-time or part-time parish catechist to build up a variety of catechetical

programmes within the parish or parishes and to encourage parental and community contact with local schools.

Without doubt there is effort involved in a partnership approach to sacramental preparation. There is also a great opportunity. With the possibility to question, to make suggestions and to work together, the adults as well as the children may once again discover the mystery inherent in the process of Christian initiation, brought about through participation in Baptism, Confirmation and the Eucharist.

Preparation Involving the Parish Community

Sacramental celebration should be a culminating moment that comes after a process of preparation of which the whole parish community is aware and involved. As liturgical scholar Aidan Kavanagh notes 'The Early Church put far more emphasis on preparation for liturgy than on liturgy itself.'[1] St Augustine was struck by the vigorous voices of the people at worship, and was so impressed indeed by their thunderous 'Amens', that this played a role in his own conversion to faith in Christ. Preparation for the sacraments, then, should involve the support of all members of the faithful in the community. The community should witness the enrolment of children for their first experience of the sacraments of Reconciliation and of Communion. During the preparatory weeks the symbolism of the sacrament could be explored and embraced in the parish, particularly perhaps at the parish's Family Mass. Such explorations should not however explain away symbols, rendering them banal. The Christian community needs to befriend its symbols and allow them speak to life, as Tad Guzie points out in *The Book of Sacramental Basics*:

> To live a symbolic life means that we have to take the step that is beyond building houses and fences and better

mousetraps. To live a symbolic life is simply to bring faith to the stuff of life, and so befriend our symbols.[2]

First-time parents, for example, benefit from the support of parish in helping them to prepare for their child's baptism. The symbols of new life and light, of anointing and communion, which dominate the sacraments of initiation, reveal their meaning when there is a lived experience of belonging to a caring, concerned and supportive Christian community. The parents' journey with their children in this way becomes a journey undertaken within the embrace of the whole Christian community. For the parish community, too, participation in the initiation of new members gives it new life and a sense of joy in the celebration of the sacraments.

Drinking from the Wellsprings of Tradition
The local parish community can learn much from tradition. Looking back and examining the practice of previous generations in faith can illuminate present and future practice. An historical analysis, such as the one provided by Neasa Ní Argadáin in her article in this volume, is very helpful in coming to a greater understanding of the meaning and power of the sacraments. Drawing from the well of tradition to reveal such meaning, may also help to re-ignite sacramental practice. This task cannot be the sole responsibility of ordained ministers or religious or indeed teachers of religious education. The Christian community must work together, coming to understand the rites of initiation as an ongoing process, a lifelong journey; a journey where one supports the other, where one celebrates with the other. The community of believers is continually called upon to breathe new life into the rites of initiation and indeed into all the sacraments. In Pope

John Paul II's apostolic letter at the close of the Great Jubilee of the year 2000, *Novo Millennio Ineunte*, he invited Christians to 'put out into the deep' (Luke 5:4).[3] The past provides key insights into the celebration of the sacraments of initiation. The invitation today is to find ways of living this initiation joyfully in the community and of setting out together on the Christian journey through life.

RENEWING OUR CELEBRATION OF THE EUCHARIST

Turning to the specific issue of parish-based preparation for first Holy Communion, four key points about the celebration of the Eucharist, derived from the experience of believers who have lived in Christ over the centuries, seem essential. If Christians are to be fully aware of their communion with God and with each other in the parish community then a renewed understanding, giving rise to a corresponding deeply felt practice, needs to emerge. Together, then, they can renew their celebration of his presence with them and their presence to each other. The second part of this article considers four themes as the focus around which a renewal of parish based preparation and celebration of the Eucharist might take place.

Sunday Mass

Sunday Mass is the most important pastoral setting in the Catholic Church.[4] In the sacramental preparation of a community's children for first Holy Communion there is an invitation to engage the whole community. The community, in turn, will become the catalyst for the young peoples' active participation at the Sunday Mass. First Holy Communion is a child's most memorable entrance into the sacramental life of the Church. As part of the child's preparation there is an opportunity to explore ways in which the Christian community sees itself gathered around the Eucharist. The Vatican's *Directory for Masses with Children* provides an interesting starting point for reflection on this when it states that catechesis for those preparing for first Holy Communion ought to cultivate those human values involved in celebrating the eucharist.[5] As a gathered community, at-one-ment is expressed in 'coming together' and 'expressing genuine sorrow' for any wrongdoings. The Word of God is 'listened to' and 'responded to' in the prayers of the faithful. The community gives 'thanks' to God the Father for sending His Son, Jesus as Saviour, who in turn offered himself as a thanksgiving sacrifice for humankind. The Body and Blood of Jesus is 'received' and finally the community 'goes forth in peace' at the end of the celebration. This 'going' is a ritual going out into the world as much as it is a practical exiting. These 'ordinary' activities take place in ordinary life. They can be explored at that level and at the same time recognised as taking the Christian beyond what is experienced as ordinary.

In Communion with Each Other

In today's modern world, society can be more an accumulation of separate individuals than a community. St Paul speaks of the Christian community as being the Body of Christ. 'As in one body we have many members, and not all the members have the same function, so we, who are many, are one body in Christ, and individually we are members one of another.' (Romans 12: 4-5). A Christian community therefore, is a society where the people are in communion with each other. To be in communion with each other calls for a shared responsibility which binds one to the other in a relationship of giving and receiving. The concept of the Church as *'communio'* was one of the central themes of renewal at Vatican II. The Church is a people made one in the communion of the Father, Son and the Holy Spirit. Each individual member must be aware of his or her own personal invitation into a relationship with the original community of the Church, the Blessed Trinity. This invitation presents the Christian with the challenge to do what Jesus did, even until death, as they journey towards God. On this journey they are nourished and sustained through participation in the Eucharist. The Eucharist unites them with God the Father, through the death and resurrection of Christ, by the grace of the Holy Spirit.

In 1970 Karl Rahner remarked that most Christians were 'mere monotheists',[6] believing in one God without focusing on the three persons of the Blessed Trinity. Certainly, one hears little sustained reflection on the Trinity. For the believing community, the invitation to share in the unity of the Trinity presents a challenge to live in a relationship of giving and receiving with God the Father, the Son and the Holy Spirit and with each other. The opportunity to observe and participate in the process with those who are preparing to receive the sacraments of initiation suggests a greater chance that the community drawn together in this way would come to more fully appreciate the treasures offered in the sacraments. 'The Church does not exist primarily for the spiritual comfort of individuals but rather to build a community that witnesses to the values that Jesus preached.'[7]

Belonging to the Parish Community

As with any development in life, changing aspects of sacramental celebrations and practice will take time. One way to begin is to remodel what is already in existence. Often, sacramental celebrations have become all too privatised. An example of this, for instance, would be baptismal celebration.

More and more baptisms are celebrated as if they were for immediate and extended family members only. The parish community does not have the opportunity to be part of the celebration. Baptismal ceremonies celebrated in such a way, accordingly, fail to touch the lives of the extended parish community.

The sacrament that regularly gathers the community together, however, is the Eucharist. The Sunday Mass involves the community in active parish participation. 'The Sunday celebration of the Lord's Day and His Eucharist is at the heart of the Church's life.'[8] Receiving the Eucharist for the first time should be a major communal celebration which involves people from all parts of the believing community rather than just the families of those who are immediately involved. It should be a 'culminating moment', a day of celebrations, coming after meticulous preparation. A sense of shared responsibility in the process of sacramental preparation by the Christian community ideally should promote a sense for the children of belonging within the local Church.

In an article entitled 'Church as Communio' Walter Kasper remarked that the danger of isolation and the misery of loneliness were never so great as in society today.[9] People are a collection of separate individuals who now, more than ever, yearn for a sense of belonging. For many young people, the rigidity of social institutions is rejected in favour of small 'base' groups that offer solidarity and almost magical solutions. The credibility of all large institutions, such as the Church, comes under intense scrutiny. Yet the cry for a sense of belonging rings clear in society today and particularly among the young. In order to answer this cry, the Church is challenged to devote both time and resources into building up the community of people who participate regularly at the Sunday Mass. This is the mission of the Church; to live life true to gospel values, to manifest shared responsibility, to belong and participate in the communion of the Trinity.

Encountering the Presence of Christ

The priest plays a crucial role in the celebration of the Eucharist. He presides over the assembly, making Christ visible in the community. He interprets the scriptures and invokes the Holy Spirit so that the bread and wine become the Body and Blood of Christ. Through the priest, Christ is made present to the community of believers. Since Vatican II, lay Catholics have become more aware of God's Word speaking to them in the scriptures. They have embraced the concept of all members of the Church being the People of God. When the community assembles together to celebrate the Eucharist, each individual shares in the presence of Christ. However strong or weak a person is, they too have the capacity to embody the presence of Christ by virtue of the fact that they are gathered together in his name. They encounter the apex of Christ's presence under the appearance of bread and wine in the Mass. Traditionally this was the only form of Christ's presence that was really highlighted. The use of the phrase 'real presence', when describing Christ's presence in the Eucharist, often led to the belief that this was the only way Christ was present in the celebration of the Mass. However, the *Catechism of the Catholic Church* states:

> This presence is called *real* – by which is not intended to exclude the other types of presence as if they could not be *real* too, but because it is presence in the fullest sense: that is to say, it is a *substantial* presence by which Christ, God and Man, makes himself wholly and entirely present.[10]

The consummate sacramental encounter with Christ is eucharistic Communion. Christians joining with Christ unite themselves with each other. They become the Body of Christ, united with God the Father by means of the death and resurrection of Christ through the grace of the Holy Spirit. This communion sanctifies and makes them holy. This point is of utmost importance and one that is often forgotten by the People of God. The sense of 'being Church', of being the 'Body of Christ' is not always appreciated or understood. A sense of sacredness towards self and towards others is often lost in a world which promotes a 'might is right' mentality. This reality deserves attention and can be explored in preparation for first Holy Communion. With the children of the community a sense of the sacredness of each person should be fostered and nourished. A sense of belonging to a community where respect for self and for the other is encouraged will promote the Church as a *whole* community, which *together* experiences the presence of Christ. Christians have to be bread for others, just as Jesus is bread given for them. Through communal sacramental preparation for first Holy Communion, the assembly gathered will come to an awareness that this ritual meal and sacrifice, the Sunday Mass, makes social and communal demands. It is not over at the final hymn. Holy Communion is nourishment and sustenance for the journey towards the final eucharistic banquet. Because this celebration offers a foretaste of human destiny, the Christian should feel the freedom to take up the challenge it presents, to act justly, to love tenderly and to walk humbly with God (Micah 6:8).

In conclusion, the sacraments of initiation celebrating full participative membership of the Catholic community should be prepared for and witnessed to within the local parish community. A deep understanding of the Sunday liturgy, of communion with each other, of belonging together within parish, and of the various possibilities of encountering the presence of Christ culminating in participation in the Eucharist is the basis upon which Holy Communion can be entered into most fully. Such a rich understanding suggests reflective commitment to parish as the ground upon which all those involved can renew their participation in the sacramental preparation of young people. Such an approach will benefit the young people in their understanding of communion with the Lord, with those who belong to their parish community and with the Church. It will also benefit the people of the parish as they grow together in communion.

Notes

1. A. Kavanagh. 'Initiation: Baptism and Confirmation' in M.J. Taylor (ed.) *The Sacraments: Readings in Contemporary Sacramental Theology* (New York: Alba House, 1981), p. 81.

2. T. Guzie, *The Book of Sacramental Basics* (New York: Paulist Press, 1981), p. 129.

3. See John Paul II, *Novo Millennio Ineunte*, Eng. trans. (2001) [online]. Available from: http://www.vatican.va/holy_father/john_paul_ii /index.htm [Accessed 10 May 2004].

4. See Sacred Congregation for Divine Worship, *Directory on Children's Masses* (London: Catholic Truth Society, 1974), par. 9.

5. See M. Drumm and T. Gunning, *A Sacramental People,* Vol. 1 (Dublin: Columba, 1999), p. 111.

6. Cited in M. P. Gallagher, 'Show Atheists the Trinity', *The Tablet,* 24 January 1998, p. 104.

7. M. Drumm and T Gunning, *A Sacramental People,* Vol. 1, p. 18.

8. *Catechism of the Catholic Church,* Eng. trans. (London: Geoffrey Chapman, 1994), par. 2177.

9. See W. Kasper, 'Church as Communio', *Communio: International Catholic Review* 13 (1986), pp. 100-117.

10. *Catechism of the Catholic Church,* par. 1374.

'GO OUT AND INVITE EVERYONE TO THE FEAST'

Liturgical Inclusion for People with Special Needs

Peg Caverley

It is a fact that people with special needs are often excluded from participating fully in society. This exclusion can also be experienced in relation to religious occasions such as the celebration of liturgy and the conferring of sacraments. If one of the keys to faith is liturgical celebration, then participation must be opened up to those who are disabled and have become marginalised in this aspect of life. Inclusion means that a community must provide opportunities for all people. It must take account of those with a disability and facilitate their full participation in all aspects of everyday society: education, employment, domestic life, recreation and also religious celebration. Inclusion as an issue is addressed more and more today, in education and in society. Although institutional churches have often sought to reach out to the disabled in a variety of ways they too are only beginning to embrace the disabled person in an inclusive manner. Belonging to a faith community is a right of people with special needs:

> The challenge of Christian remembrance is to perform
> the same gestures of sharing and intimacy, to respect and
> reverence the things common to life, to stand in awe

before the sacred and in trust against evil, in settings and groups where divisions and discriminations have no entry.[1]

If inclusion is valid for education it is also relevant for the spiritual development of children with special needs as their greatest suffering is to be made to feel different or useless.[2] This article addresses particular issues associated with liturgical inclusion for people with special needs by reflecting on the results of an initiative undertaken in 2002-2003 which researched the appropriateness of an inclusive approach, encouraging the full participation of young people with special needs within the worshipping community.

Roscrea Parish and School Initiative

The study, addressing issues of integration and inclusion in liturgical settings, was carried out at St Cronan's Roman Catholic parish, Roscrea, Co. Tipperary, in conjunction with the local St Anne's Special Needs School. The study assessed the attitudes of twenty parishioners toward the special needs population.[3] The special needs group consisted of seven students from Class 7 at St Anne's who took an active part in four specifically designed parish liturgies as part of their preparation for Confirmation. It was hypothesised that there would be a more positive attitude on the part of the mainstream parish community toward the special needs population as a result of the inclusive liturgies and secondly, that there would be advantages for the special needs population in areas of independence, decision-making, sharing space, forming relationships and contributing to the community.

The special needs population was measured by behavioural observation using John O'Brien's 'Principles for

Normalization'.[4] These are based on five values experienced by all including those with disabilities: making choices, sharing ordinary places, growing in relationship, contributing and dignity and respect.

Making Choices
As part of the study the innate right and freedom of making choices was given to each of the seven students. The student had:

- The choice of whether to attend Mass or not
- The choice of selecting one's own seat
- The choice of receiving Holy Communion
- The choice of lighting a vigil candle
- The choice of participating in a more active way within the liturgy.

At each of our liturgies there were no fewer than four of the students. Usually all seven attended, however. The students viewed attending the liturgy as an outing and as a preparation for Confirmation. After March, they could select their own seat, usually sitting in twos, within four to five pews of each other. They all received Holy Communion at each Mass in their own time with the exception of Anthony, a non-Catholic, who would approach the altar for a blessing. Each student lit vigil candles and offered a prayer for an intention. Students gladly volunteered to:

- Read paraphrased Scripture
- Lead prayers of the faithful
- Serve Mass
- Sing Responsorial Psalm

- Sign the Our Father
- Present Gifts at the Offertory.

Making choices gave each student more independence, with positive effect, and the confidence to make further decisions.

Sharing Ordinary Places
'Sharing Ordinary Places is one of the most powerful ways of reducing the perceived difference regarding people with disabilities.'[5] St Cronan's Church is the parish church with which St Anne's Special Needs School is associated. Although 90 per cent of the students live outside the parish it was deemed important by school, parish and parents that the students felt part of this parish. The students became familiar with the choir gallery, sanctuary, and devotional altars as well as with the Advent sacred space, Lenten sacred space and Easter garden. They moved independently within the church at appropriate times. Students were also encouraged to find these places in their own parish churches.

Growing in relationships
It was evident that during the period of the four adapted liturgies each student developed a relationship with other members of the congregation. This was evident by the friendly exchanges before and after Mass, at the Sign of Peace, when Confirmation candidates distributed prayer cards and later when they received Confirmation cards from once unknown parishioners.

Contributing
Contributions to the liturgy ranged from actions such as the ringing of the bell at the Consecration and extending a hand at

the Sign of Peace to the more significant actions of Reading and singing the Responsorial Psalm. A particularly striking reaction within one of the inclusive liturgies concerned the praying of the Our Father. The students from St Anne's School signed the Our Father which meant the priest had to recite the prayer much more slowly than usual. Members of the congregation remarked later how meaningful it was to experience the prayer prayed in gesture and at a slower pace. As Brett Webb-Mitchell points out: 'Gestures are important to our human life in general and to the Christian culture in particular.'[6] A dozen simple hand signs proved to be both powerful and meaningful.

Dignity and Respect

All of the aforementioned principles (making choices, sharing ordinary places, contributing, and growing in relationships) increase the dignity and respect of the young person involved. This was most noted by the manner in which the students conducted themselves while in the parish church. Each student was quiet, reverent and attentive. After the liturgy, the students were affirmed by parishioners and by the celebrant. On returning to school, they were able to relay in picture or word something seen or heard during the Mass. This would not have been possible if mutual acceptance and acknowledgement of each member in the community, the prerequisites for social integration,[7] were not present.

The Effects and Implications of the Study

The integration of the special needs population at St Cronan's Church significantly influenced the attitudes of the mainstream population. The results from the survey indicated that the liturgies had a positive effect on the sample of twenty parishioners surveyed from the mainstream population. Changes in attitudes were demonstrated to have occurred because of the inclusion of the students from the special school. Their presence contributed to an awareness in the community of the abilities of a group of people labelled disabled.

The students from Class 7 also benefited from the integration as observed and recorded by their teacher and special needs assistants. Students displayed an improvement in social skills as a result of their inclusion in the wider community. Making choices, sharing ordinary places, contributing and growing in relationships increased the dignity and respect of each young person involved. 'The experience of dignity or status, or to have people show respect, is a positive one for all of us.'[8]

The results of the study indicate a statistically very significant change in the attitudes toward people with disabilities,[9] showing that attitudes can be changed through integration. Support is necessary to facilitate a change in attitudes, address fears and provide the skills required to meet the specific needs of people with a wider range of individual differences. Pamela Wickham-Searl proposes that, as a result of the inclusion of people with special needs:

- Churches will become more knowledgeable about disabilities
- Churches will become more imaginative in the various aspects of congregational life
- Churches will become more patient and tolerant of differences
- Churches will become more intimate as they give and receive support to one another
- Churches will become more resilient and not easily threatened by the new and different.[10]

There is evidence that the Church is striving to be more inclusive. In spite of positive public attitudes, however, people with physical and learning disabilities continue to be excluded from mainstream society in general and houses of worship in particular. Parishes today are on 'fast forward' trying to deal with and delegate the ministries that have been opened up and are being embraced by enthusiastic laity. Music Ministries, Readers, Ministers of the Eucharist, Youth Masses, Youth Choirs, Children's and Family Liturgies, the Rite of Christian Initiation of Adults, Counselling and Parish Councils are running full force and in many cases without the presence of people with special needs and disabilities. The Church can be a leader in setting an example of inclusive acceptance: 'We, as members of the Christian faith community should be at the forefront of this movement to integrate disabled persons into our Church's life.'[11]

The key to integration is inclusion and the key to faith is liturgy. 'Incorporating people into the assembly who previously were excluded redefines the very character of the assembly.'[12] Inclusive and integrated liturgies provide an opportunity to recognise the imperfections and limitations of all. Through them life and vulnerability are linked and the individual's need for others is highlighted. This inter-connectedness is a reminder to us that Christianity is a relational faith. People with special needs like to relate. They are in relation with many 'others'. They may require, for example, home help, bus escort, principal, teacher, classroom assistant, school nurse, occupational therapist, speech therapist and physical therapist. These relationships are formed in addition to family, extended family, neighbours, friends and hopefully the parish community. Consequently people with special needs touch the lives of many people giving them opportunities to change the heart and attitudes of others: 'All of us are in relationship with others, the universe and the mystery called God.'[13] As attitudes change, faith communities can be imagined that will extinguish fear and teach the skills necessary to ensure successful integration.

Now is the Time: Taking the Initiative

In the wake of the 'European Year of People with Disabilities' and the Special Olympics in Ireland, celebrated in 2003, this is an opportune time to harness good will and unite people who have expertise and vision. Within the Church, dioceses should review their response to people with special needs. They should research the needs of such people in relation to diocese and parish and develop ways of including, integrating and using the talents and insights of people with disabilities. People with special needs should have a place on parish councils as well as in church assemblies.

A Time to Reflect

How can the 'ably different' be involved in the everyday life of the Church, enhance their spirituality and find acceptance? How can obstacles to inclusion be removed: disrespectful attitudes, lack of awareness and lack of organisation. The Christian community must respond to the disabled, not out of charity, pity or even Christian duty, but because, in taking a closer look at itself, the limitations of all members are recognised. The Christian call is attractive but challenging. The grace to sustain the Church on its journey is, however, freely offered by God. This grace is available for all; the grace of gratitude for roots, for family and culture, for friends and for people with disabilities. Churches and tables will remain incomplete until everyone is welcomed to the feast.

A Time to Imagine

The Church can begin to re-imagine the world by starting with the local community, with the local parish. Imagination is needed in order that parishes might embrace the special needs community that has so much to offer. Faith can be refuelled and replenished by sharing experiences with people who have special needs. The first exercise might be a survey of the local parish to access the needs of such people and suggest ideas for their accommodation within Church. Parishes might then appoint parish community workers to minister to the spiritual and pastoral needs of people with disabilities. This requires well-organised, informed and committed Christians at diocesan and parish level working to find ways that will allow those with disabilities to participate in parish liturgies and organisations.

A Time to Reach Out

As the key to faith is liturgy, gathering around the Lord's Table is a fitting place to begin. Liturgy is vital to the identity of the Church. New liturgies for new times are essential. 'One of the great sources of renewal in the Church has always come from the edge, the margins.'[14] A community develops through its experience of liturgy. Liturgies, therefore, should be accessible to all who wish to participate in the life of the Church.

Experiences of people with special needs can touch the other person deeply. Such an experience may be like a soft tap on the shoulder to make one aware of the presence of the other. Sometimes it can come as a shove making one move in a direction not considered before, a direction that would aid the integration and inclusion of people with special needs in society. A person may also experience an actual push, throwing one into direct and daily contact, working with people who have special needs, developing perhaps into a career. Eventually, one might, at some point, find oneself entering into a way of life with them. A connection with God has been made. God has been waiting, waiting to be recognised in the face of the person with disabilities. The experience, the gestures and the symbols used when working with people with special needs is grounded in sound theology. Theology must engage in a critical reflection on human experience. Based on that reflection it must suggest a response wholeheartedly undertaken with a Christian spirit. Human beings are brought together and discover wholeness by embracing each other. For people, in fact, need each other.

And Time Moves On – A Year Later
A year later, as I write, the students continue to attend a weekday liturgy. They are now spreading their wings in the parish. After Mass one day each week, some of the students set the tables in the Legion Hall. The kettle is boiled and cakes and scones made in Home Economics class are served to parishioners who come in for a chat. The 'coffee stop' provides an opportunity for students to hone their pre-vocational skills and to show they have something to give to the parish. The parishioners, too, are glad of this social element. This feeling is shared with the students, as is the laughter, something that is always genuine and does not lie.

Organisation is needed to capture the imagination, experience and expertise of people who can open doors and open hearts to include people who are 'ably different'.[15] The Special Olympics slogan, 'Share the Feeling', should be allowed to join the myriad of other slogans that roar at us daily. When our hearts open our doors will open too; not just physical doors, but doors of opportunity to share the everyday experiences many of us take so much for granted.

When we can 'just do it'
we will experience how it is 'good for you'
and thus 'share the feeling'.

Notes

1. D.N. Power, 'Households of Faith in the Coming Church', M.Warren (ed.) *Source Book for Modern Catechetics,* Vol. 2 (Winona, MN: St Mary's Press, 1987), p. 171.

2. See J. Vanier, *Eruption to Hope* (New York: Paulist Press, 1971), p. 39.

3. In the study Harold Yucker's 'Attitudes Towards Disabled Person Scale' was used. See H.E. Yucker, *Attitudes Towards Persons with Disabilities* (New York: Springer Publishing, 1980).

4. Cited in B. McCormack, M. Rafferty and C. Lynch, *Values to Practice: A Practical Course in Normalisation for Front Line Staff,* (Dublin: Open Road, St Michael's House Training, 1990), p. 18.

5. B. McCormack, M. Rafferty and C. Lynch, *Values to Practice,* p. 18.

6. B. Webb-Mitchell, *Unexpected Guests at God's Banquet: Welcoming People with Disabilities Into the Church* (New York: Crossroad, 1994), p. 159.

7. See A. Kakkioniemi, 'Church and Social Integration of Disabled People', *Panorama: International Journal of Comparative Religious Education and Values* 13/1(2001).

8. B. McCormack, M. Rafferty and C. Lynch, *Values to Practice,* p. 15

9. The 'Attitudes Toward Disabled Persons Scale' indicated a very significant change in the attitudes toward people with disabilities ($p=0.0020$).

10. Cited in B. Webb-Mitchell, *Unexpected Guests at God's Banquet,* p. 126-127

11. S. Hall, *Into the Christian Community* (Washington DC: National Catholic Educational Association, 1982), p. 10.

12. D. Bergant, 'Come, Let Us Go to the Mountain of the Lord', E. Foley (ed.) *Developmental Disabilities and Sacramental Access: New Paradigm for Sacramental Encounters* (Collegeville, MN: The Liturgical Press, 1994), p. 29.

13. M. Drumm, *Passage to Pasch* (Dublin: Columba, 1998), p. 123.
14. M. Drumm, *Passage to Pasch*, p. 133.
15. M.A. Giglotti, 'Opening Hearts, Doors and Minds: So That All May Worship' National Organization for Disabilities, Interfaith Conference, Cliften Park, New York, 3 December 2000.

WHAT CAN THE SPIRITUALITY OF THE CELTS CONTRIBUTE TO SPIRITUALITY TODAY?

Maura Boyle-McNally

The interest today in Celtic spirituality is considerable. The Celts were a creative, imaginative people, who shared a common culture and a common language. Their cultural and linguistic experiences set them apart from the Latin West and coloured the form of Christianity adopted in Ireland. The current interest in all things Celtic from jewellery to the economy might only be of marginal interest to the Christian. The spirituality of the early Celtic Church, however, produced a unique Christian blossoming from a formerly pagan culture, which continues to intrigue and inspire in areas such as art, music, crafts, literary works, and in the growth of modern Celtic communities and retreat houses. There is little doubt that the life and times of the Celts have been greatly romanticised in modern times. It is still possible, however, to piece together a picture of the beliefs, practices and priorities of the Christian Church as it developed among the Celts in Ireland. What emerges is a picture of a vibrant outward looking Church that has much to teach us today.

A Spiritual Heritage

It is thought that the Celts settled in Ireland around 500 BC. According to Julius Caesar, the Celts were to a great extent a religious people greatly immersed in worship and ritual at particular times of the year, especially during the change of the seasons. They also believed in an afterlife and the supernatural. For the Celts, the soul was immortal, and death simply a passing from one world to the next. In Celtic mythology human beings were considered capable of entering or leaving the burial mound or sídh as a bird, particularly at Samhain. For this reason birds became sacred to the Celts and later appeared in the decoration of the great gospel Book of Kells. Druids were seen as intermediaries with the spirit world and as such had the power to safeguard people from the maliciousness of evil spirits. The role of the Druid was readily taken over by the Christian monk.

The Celtic world was pervaded by a multiplicity of gods and goddesses of whom the names of two hundred have been recorded. Lugh was a widely revered deity in the Celtic world renowned for the splendour of his countenance. His feast was celebrated at Lunasa at the beginning of August. With little difficulty, the old Celtic gods were re-presented among the Christian saints and the mighty figure of Lugh was soon identified with the figure of the archangel Michael. Shrines to this warrior angel are to be found on mountain heights in Cornwall, Brittany and on the Skellig rock off the coast of Kerry.

Fertility gods and goddesses also abound in Celtic tradition, including Cernunnos the Antlered, depicted on the Gundestrup Cauldron, who was also the god of the hunt, and of the untamed forces of nature. He is seen as the primary consort of the Great Mother Goddess of Earth. Their union celebrated at Bealtaine, represents the union of male and female, the conscious and unconscious mind, the positive and negative in life. Cernunnos is often depicted holding a snake, a symbol that also came to signify the Resurrection, because it lives on – renewed after shedding its skin.

Cernunnos dies at Samhain, the beginning of winter, only to be reborn anew at Imbolg the start of spring. The cycle of death and birth follows the seasons of growth with the waxing and waning of sunlight. This eternal cycle of nature and the seasons, depicted in the spirals of Celtic art, came to symbolise the intertwining of God and humanity, spirit and matter. They were used later to illuminate the great gospel books of Kells and Durrow and to decorate sacred vessels and high crosses. The importance of the sun and the seasons in the life of the Celts may well have been kept alive in the circle incorporated in the Irish high crosses, which Joyce says 'may represent the sun, a vestige of old Celtic worship … as pagan beliefs were adapted to Christianity.'[1]

The goddess called Brigit, daughter of the chief god Daghda, also gained admittance into Christian sainthood woven into the story of St Brigid, Abbess of Kildare. She too was associated with fertility, healing, crafts, poetry and learning. The Celts revered motherhood, and the association of their gods and goddesses with fertility reflected their life-honouring reverence for mother earth as a source of life. The image of the goddess is an important affirmation of the spirituality, power and sacredness of women, often considered by some as being overlooked in the Roman Church. Such an image represents 'an ancient people's wonderment with the awesome mystery of the fact that life emerges from the body of a woman.'[2] She represented the roles of creator, mother, virgin, maid, and was the source of birth and rebirth. Many pagan deities were represented in threes as was the goddess Brigit. This Trinitarian consciousness permeated Celtic spirituality and allowed for an easy acceptance of the Christian doctrine of the Trinity.

Religious Sites

The best-preserved aspects of the Celtic belief systems are their religious sites, which involved manipulation and enhancement of the natural landscape including groves, lakes and watery places used for worship. Most rituals and ceremonies were carried on outdoors. Trees were highly regarded, particularly the oak, which was seen as sacred and life giving. Standing stones were erected to mark or 'socialise' the environment,[3] or to solemnise an already sacred area. The form of the circle occurs widely in magic and religion as a protective device, or a technique for controlling the cosmos, and survived into the Christian era. 'A common ritual practice was that of the Caim. Celts would draw a circle around themselves with a finger as they prayed to the Trinity to encircle and protect them.'[4]

In Celtic belief, natural waters – springs, rivers, lakes and ponds – contained the souls of indwelling spirits, which were to be acknowledged and nurtured. Most Irish rivers have female names and medieval literature describes how these names belonged to the goddesses of the underworld. Wells were later adopted by Christianity and associated with the saints. Water, an important symbol for the Celts, was also an important symbol for Christians who understood Christ as 'the living water' (John 4:10). 'The significance of a convenient water-supply for baptism was very real to the early missionaries'[5] giving the holy well a specifically Christian orientation. As a place where the sun retreated at night, the well symbolised for the Celts the inner light of life as contrasted with the outer light of the visible world. The waters represented a hidden source of wisdom, and the well itself was understood as a channel from the unconscious to the conscious. The association of the wells with light has strong echoes of Christianity where Christ is acclaimed 'the light of the world' (John 8:12). For the Celts just as the sunlight emerges from the well at daybreak, dispelling darkness, so dim eyes can be illumined once more by the sacred waters. Related to this is the traditional belief in the power of holy springs to cure eye diseases. One particular well reputed to have this cure is Lady's Well, Mulhuddart, Co. Dublin, while another, at nearby Diswellstown, also had the cure. Here pilgrims came to the well on May eve, the old Celtic festival of Bealtaine. They would bathe their eyes with a rag dipped in the water, which was then left hanging on a tree beside the well.

The Christian adaptation to Celtic culture can be witnessed in many public 'well devotions' in Ireland to this day. The first Sunday in September is the pattern day (a day on or near the feast of the 'Patron' saint associated with an area when prayer rituals are performed), for St. Ciarán's well at Clonmacnoise. Pilgrims follow the pilgrimage pathways and hang offerings on a thornless hawthorn bush, or throw them in the well. Another of St. Ciarán's wells is at Castlekieran in Co. Meath. Pennick records: 'Pilgrims go there with torches at midnight on the first Sunday in August, on or near Lughnasa, the old Celtic festival of the solar God Lugh.'[6] A large number of 'patterns', particularly those associated with mountain sites, take place at the time of the old Celtic Lughnasa feast, now usually celebrated on the last Sunday in July. Climbing Croagh Patrick in Co Mayo is an example of this.

The 'turas deiseal', or walk 'sunwise' is also carried out as part of Christian rituals to the present day when people walk in circular motion around a holy well, statue or church reciting the rosary:

> When circumambulation is employed in ritual practices, it is considered correct to move in the same direction as the sun. It was customary in more recent Irish tradition

for a funeral cortege to walk right-handedly around the cemetery before interring the corpse there.[7]

Celtic Spirituality for Today

Spirituality as a journey into the self and beyond self, the journey to wholeness, is as much a feature of Christian life today as it was in the past. There is an ongoing search for a holistic spirituality, a new way of seeing and approaching reality, based on a fully integrated self, integrated too with the wider world. Celtic Christianity is being rediscovered as a vital resource for a creation-celebrating and a life-honouring spirituality. Some of the particular features of the early Celtic Church may be of help on the journey to wholeness. By connecting again with the Celtic Christian tradition, the home, the school and the parish, within their own context and together, may provide the individual and the Christian community with a deeper sense of self, a renewed vision of Church, and openness to the richness of tradition as a possible source of new life. Each new generation deserves an opportunity to learn from the faith experience of previous generations so that they can begin to shape their spiritual and religious way of life within the context of the people to whom they belong.

Reconnecting with Nature

In Celtic spirituality the divine is revealed in and through the natural world. Many alienating dualisms associated with modern Western culture – the immanence and transcendence of God, the separation of humankind from creation, body from soul, male from female, feelings and emotions from rationality and logic – cause a disconnectedness which affects our perception of reality, and are in need of repair. Celtic spirituality lowers the barriers of separation between the human and the divine. It establishes a sense of connectedness with the earth and creates a sense of being at home with nature. The world is infused with the sense of the all-pervading presence of God. 'The elements sound and show forth the knowledge of God through the work that they do.'[8] Nature was mystery for the Celts. Rivers, mountains, wells, as we have seen, were all understood as being imbued with the spirits of gods and goddesses. The druids sang incantations for protection against unknown forces showing an awareness of the power of God, an understanding of the nature of the spirit world and of the presence of malign forces against which protection was required. Even though humans are separated from the rest of creation by being created in God's image (Gen 1:27) human dependence on the natural world can never be overlooked. A position of privilege means a responsibility for proper stewardship of earth's gifts. As pollution, and exploitation damage the earth it becomes more difficult today to see the presence of God mediated through it. There is great urgency, therefore, to regain respect for the earth while there is still time to do so.

In Touch With the Feminine

Celtic pagan society honoured the feminine, in its goddesses and in its conception of the earth as mother. The goddess Eriu or Eire gave her name to Ireland after giving her land to the Milesian Celts on their arrival in Ireland. Aspects of the feminine, and of its particular awareness of God, needs to be reawakened and affirmed in the Church. Western religious inheritance has often led to mistrust of the senses and of feelings rather than to the recognition of their validity. Women generally held an equal position to men in Celtic society, and this was accepted also in the early Celtic Christian Church it seems. An abbot or abbess was the administrative leader of the community leaving the sacramental and evangelical functions to bishop and priest. There was no clergy/lay divide, or male/female divide. All fulfilled their role on an equal footing. There is also evidence of women's role in the Church and 'of groups of deaconesses called Conhospitae, who had a liturgical role in the Eucharist.'[9] The Celtic Church did not totally separate the sexes, nor did it display the fear of sexuality that dominated the Western Church later on. In fact, mixed monasteries were commonplace. The more the Celtic Church conformed to the Roman way, however, the more patriarchal it became. Women's role in the church appears to have diminished gradually after the Synod of Whitby in 664, which saw the defeat of the Celtic Church on the issues of the date of Easter and the tonsure. Ironically the Synod was held in East Anglia at the monastery of a famous Celtic abbess, St Hilda. Celtic Christian spirituality invites Christianity today to once again celebrate the dignity, value and sacredness of the feminine in society and in the Church, and respond to its presence in an appropriate way in the liturgy.

Intimacy with God

The image people possess of God greatly affects how they relate both to God and to the natural world. One cannot relate to someone who is presented as distant or as being too remote to be interested in the realities of human life. Here much can be learned from the attitude of the Celtic peoples to God. The Celtic Christians' strong affinity with the mysticism and teachings of St John taught them always to see God in relation to the whole of creation and life. God is a God of love:

John underlines the fact that Jesus is the object of all the love of the Father, and is sent on a mission of salvation. He had not been sent to judge, or to condemn, he had come to save.[10]

Celtic Christians modelled God on their notion of a tribal leader or chief, who was familiar in their rural society, and who had a personal and protective interest in their everyday affairs. The awesome Creator of the universe was a protective and nurturing high chief. Living and praying became inseparable. Every activity, whether grinding corn or weaving cloth, was committed to God in prayer. As the life of God was intertwined with the life of his creatures so everything was put under his care. Blessings were an intrinsic part of life and were spontaneously recited on every occasion from birth to death. The *Lorica*, a form of prayer based on a pagan charm against natural phenomena and evil spirits, developed as a Christian prayer focused on the Celtic understanding of God as interested in every aspect of life. It celebrated God the creator, and all the elements of God's creation: 'I arise today, through the strength of heaven, light of sun, radiance of moon, ... depth of sea, stability of earth, firmness of rock.'[11] The invocation of the forces of nature, used in the *Lorica*, is not common outside the Celtic tradition.

Because God was conceived not as remote or distant but as an immanent figure, many prayers contain warm endearing expressions of God's immanent presence. The poems of Blathmac (*c.* 750)[12] honour Our Lady and her Son speaking with great tenderness and humanity. The poet asks Mary to come to him that he might lament with her the death of her beautiful Son and console her heart. The poet suggests that when our Lord after His death returned to heaven and 'when the household of heaven welcomed their true heart, Mary, your beautiful Son broke into tears in their presence.'[13] That spirit of gentleness and familial intimacy in prayer is evident in many prayers and poems of the time. In our time people need to see again the presence of God in all that happens to them, in order to pray. Celtic spirituality invites us to look for God in the most ordinary and the dullest of contexts. The words of George McLeod, founder of the Iona Community, 'show us the glory in the grey',[14] which are found in one of his prayers, are particularly apt here.

Living as Community

The Celtic Christian Church, which took over from pagan Druidism, was a church dominated by monasteries and abbots rather than by dioceses and bishops as in the Roman model. This monastic tradition can be traced back to the hermits of Egypt who sought to become closer to God through the solitary life. People flocked to the desert after the conversion of the Roman Empire in the fourth century, to seek guidance from hermits like Paul of Thebes and his disciple Anthony of Egypt. The appearance of Paul and Anthony on several Irish high crosses, such as Muireadach's Cross at Monasterboice, the crosses at Moone and Kells, and the two high crosses at Castledermot,[15] indicates awareness and an appreciation of the Eastern origins of the monastic tradition among the Celtic monks. The type of fierce asceticism and penance practised in Egypt, Palestine and Syria was often referred to in Ireland as 'green martyrdom' and was seen as a way to identify with Jesus in his sufferings. 'White martyrdom,' which referred to going into voluntary exile, was seen as another way of expressing commitment to Christ: 'As Jesus let go of his divinity to embrace humanity so the monk would let go of his beloved land to follow Christ.'[16] Celtic monks renounced the world, and took themselves off to remote places to be near God, some of them even setting off to Europe and beyond. Many monasteries were established on remote and beautiful islands around the coast of Ireland such as Skellig Michael in Co Kerry, Inisbofin Co Mayo, and the Aran Islands. Beautiful wilderness areas on mountain tops, or beside the sea, lakes, rivers or wells were also sites for Celtic monasteries, such as Glendalough and Clonmacnoise, just as such places were sacred to the Celts in pre-Christian pagan Ireland. Many monastic settlements, in fact, included the word 'desert' in the Irish version of their name, for example Dysart, near Thomastown, Co Kilkenny, Disert Diarmada, the Irish for Castledermot, Co Kildare, and Dysart O'Dea, Co Clare. This probably originated after the Céile Dé movement in the eighth century when a 'desert area' for contemplation was provided close to the monastery.

Listening to the Word of God
The Celtic Church was rooted in scripture. The bible was the basic textbook for all learning and education. A rediscovery of the Word of God, as a powerful source of nourishment for the spiritual life, is therefore suggested by reference to early Celtic Christian spirituality. At the same time, when reading the texts a hermeneutic of suspicion needs to be embraced, capable, for instance, of analysing patriarchal interests. Lucy Tatman, speaking of Sophia, alerts us to the feminine face of God:

> There was Wisdom, and she was present everywhere with all the intensity and all the desire of all there was. And once the Word was spoken she and she alone dived into the spaces between the words, blessing the silence out of which new worlds are born. Now, as it was at the beginning, Wisdom is hearing all creation into speech.[17]

Sophia or Wisdom, suggestive of themes associated with the Mother Goddess of the Celts, offers new and enriching possibilities for re-examining what the bible has to say to today's world.

The Celtic love of scripture, particularly St John's writings and the psalms, is evidenced by the care and dedication in copying texts, by the proliferation of art work and illuminated manuscripts and by the scenes from scripture to be found on the great stone high crosses. John's teachings moulded the Celtic Christian tradition: 'John's way of seeing makes room for an open encounter with the Light of life, wherever it is found.'[18] His is a life-affirming spirituality. It is based in a love for God whose immanent presence is all around, who is interested and involved in all that is done, and who has come among us so that 'we may have life and have it to the full' (John 10:10). John's vision, and so therefore the Celtic Christian vision, demonstrates a readiness to delight in the sensory and in the closeness of affection. In his account of the woman who anointed Jesus with oil, John remarks that 'the house was filled with the fragrance of the perfume' (John 12:3). The Johannine tradition encourages the Christian to understand that the sensual has a place in spirituality. The sense of touch, a mode of healing used repeatedly by Jesus in his ministry, highlights the need for intimacy and closeness in coming to wholeness. This reasserting of the power of senses in sacramental life communicates that truth and understanding can come in a non-verbal way.

Supported in Friendship: *Ainmchairdeas*
There existed in the Celtic Church the very important institution of spiritual advisers, strongly influenced by the desert Christians of the East, and known as soul-friends or

ainmchairde. Each monk or nun had his or her own spiritual guide or anamchara, to whom they could open their heart. This type of ministry was open to lay people as well, men and women alike. We are told that Colmcille had a female soul-friend called Ercnat who was an embroidress and dressmaker. A reference by St Brigid of Kildare to this ministry, found in the early ninth century *Martyrology of Oengus the Culdee,* attests to its importance: 'anyone without a soul friend is like a body without a head; is like the water of a polluted lake.' Many new opportunities for soul friendships are presented today, both for individuals and groups, particularly as streams of the world's cultures merge together. The pilgrim Church, encounters many fellow travellers who, even though they are outside the visible body of the Church, are 'people of good will in whose hearts grace works in an unseen way.'[19] Christian communities are called to soul friendships of communication and cultural exchange with such people on their journey to wholeness and solidarity.

Ruled by Ritual and Rhythm
Ritual and rhythm played an important role in the prayer life of the Celtic peoples and many prayers were repeated over and over in rhythmic fashion. French philosopher Paul Riceour speaks of the imagination as a door half open, through which one can enter by means of music, art, the visual and the sensual.[20] Rita Guare adds:

> 'The imagination is the bridge of possibility where we can find depth in the ordinary. By liberating the imagination, we can pursue paths of transcendent knowledge and restore the unity of knowing and living.'[21]

For the Celts, more in tune with the rhythms of nature than are their post-modern counterparts, certain places such as groves, trees, islands, and certain times such as dawn, dusk, equinox and solstice, were significant to ritual. Various forms of behaviour such as fasting, being silent, touching, opened the door to a heightened awareness of human experience, and had the 'capacity to bring us to a different threshold where we can see things in another way.'[22] In our own time fragrance, candles, incense, oils, all have the power to contribute in a similar way, enhancing sacramental and liturgical ritual. The Celtic tradition offers a wealth and richness of ritual and rhythm that can be drawn upon to nurture Christian faith today. For Celtic peoples, ritual and movement were as important as words. Walking and processing were common forms of devotion as were pilgrimages. They pointed to the need to pray with the whole body. These processions were often accompanied by repetitive prayers, chants and litanies, which had a soothing effect on the mind, and a unifying effect on the whole praying group, providing a sense of unity of purpose, and building up the whole community of believers. The relatively recent popularity of the Taizé chants and prayers among the young demonstrates the benefits of this form of prayer.

Cleansed by Silence and Penance

As well as involvement in public worship the Christian is called to develop a personal relationship with God. One cannot do this unless a place and a time are found for God in one's life. Celtic monks sought out 'thin places' where they could be alone and find God. Silence was an important discipline in the monastic tradition. Those immersed in today's busy world of constant noise, activity, schedules and meeting deadlines can learn much from the early Celtic Christians concerning a sense of balance in one's lifestyle. Silence forces the human person into a heightened awareness of self, evoking a sense of gratitude for God's gifts. In silence a unity of truth and a feeling of connectedness that is deeper than words can be sensed.

Asceticism was practised in the Celtic Christian Church seeking to find wholeness and fulfilment through restraint. Fasting was seen as a means of gaining redress, both in the spiritual realm as well as in the law. So central was this practice of fasting in society that the practice has given its name to three of the Irish weekdays, Ceadaoin meaning first fast, Déardaoin 'between fasts' and Aoine, 'the fast.' Many of the extreme penitential exercises, including fasting, walking barefoot and deprivation of sleep are associated even today with pilgrimage to St Patrick's Purgatory in Lough Derg Co. Donegal. There were three major fasts in the Celtic Church, forty days before Easter, Whit-sun and Christmas. This compared with a single Roman fast at Lent. An appreciation of the values of fasting and silence, important elements of monastic prayer life, may prove difficult to recover in a culture of constant noise, affluence, self-fulfilment and instant satisfaction. Nevertheless, there is evidence that many, through dieting, working out, or efforts to conquer addictions are seeking freedom from all that holds the body in captivity. Celtic spirituality affirms the place of discipline, restraint and simplicity in daily life.

An Integrated Holistic Spirituality
The Celtic Church understood healing as a total experience, affecting all of life: 'Body cannot be healed apart from the soul, and neither can be healed apart from God.'[23] Celtic spirituality calls for openness to healing and reconciliation in every area of our being, acknowledging that disintegration in any one area has detrimental effects on the rest of life. There is no

dichotomy between body and soul. 'Healing means reuniting that which is estranged, giving a centre to what is split, overcoming the split between God and ourselves, ourselves and the world, as well as the split within ourselves.'[24] Celtic Christian spirituality was holistic in that it embraced the mind in its love of learning; the heart in its love of poetry, nature, art and music; the body in its dedication to work, penance, pilgrimage, prayer, fasting, the Word of God and the Eucharist. A contemporary spirituality should promote this sense of balance, integrating the spiritual and the material in daily life.

A Celtic vision for the future not only calls for an integrated world, but for an integrated and fully alive self based in healthy self-esteem, resting 'not on any external criteria but on grasping the reality that we are beloved by God, and are in a relationship of love with God.'[25] The God of the Celtic Christian vision is the God of wholeness, who in Jesus accepted human life. By taking up home within the experience of being human, God esteems humankind, additionally God redeems the world and its peoples, giving human life new dignity and value.

'You are precious in my eyes, honoured, and I love you.'
(Isaiah 43:4)

Conclusion

Memory holds within it the identity of a people and has the power to direct them along new paths, changing history: 'Memory can creatively interrupt the present and in doing so has the capacity to awaken hope in alternative styles of individual and social existence.'[26] As the rich tradition and heritage available from the Celtic Church is remembered today, a new awareness opens up of the redeeming, healing wholeness presented there. We are enabled to visualise a renewed Church, offering new possibilities for a future built on the best of what our experience tells us we can be. The young are the future. Religious education textbooks in schools should provide them with an awareness of their rich ancestry, reflecting the Celtic and Christian traditions of Ireland. Teachers, as well as parents and those involved in parish ministries, should be conscious of and, ideally, immersed in that tradition convinced of its value and reaching out to pass on to a new generation a spirituality that connects us all with a vision greater than ourselves. Reconciled with God, with nature, with our tradition and with each other, we can learn from our past to live in the present, knowing the blessing of being Celtic and Christian and open to God's revelation each and everyday.

Notes

1. T. Joyce, *Celtic Christianity: A Sacred Tradition, A Vision of Hope* (New York: Orbis Books, 1998), p. 77.
2. K. Zappone, *The Hope for Wholeness*, p.93, cited in A. Holton, *A Liberating Spirituality for Religious Educators* (Lima, Ohio: Wyndham Hall Press, 2002).
3. See D. Ó hÓgáin, *The Sacred Isle: Belief and Religion in Pre-Christian Ireland* (Cork: Collins Press, 1999), p. 2.
4. T. Joyce, *Celtic Christianity*, p. 26.
5. D. O hÓgáin *The Sacred Isle*, p. 214.
6. N. Pennick, *Celtic Sacred Landscapes* (London: Thames and Hudson, 1996), p. 69.
7. D. Ó hÓgáin *The Sacred Isle* p. 27.
8. L. Hardinge, *The Celtic Church in Britain*, p. 59, quoted in E. De Waal, *Every Earthly Blessing: Rediscovering the Celtic Tradition* (1991), reprinted (Harrisbourg PA: Moorehouse Publishing, 1999), p. 57.
9. T. Joyce, *Celtic Christianity*, p. 22.
10. W.J. Harrington, *John: Spiritual Theologian - The Jesus of John*, (Dublin: Columba, 1999), p. 36.
11. D. Hyde, *Religious Songs 11*, p. 47, cited in E. De Waal, *Every Earthly Blessing*, p. xxi.

12. See J. Carney *The Poems of Blathmac* (Dublin: Educational Company of Ireland, 1964).

13. See D. Ó Laoghaire, 'Celtic Spirituality', C. Jones, G. Wainwright, and E. Yarnold (eds.) *The Study of Spirituality* (London: SPCK, 1986), p. 218. See also D. Ó Laoghaire 'An Introduction to Celtic Spirituality' [online]. Available from http://www.orthodoxireland.com/history/celticspirituality/view

14. G. MacLeod, 'The Glory of the Grey', J.P. Newell, *The Whole Earth*, p. 14 cited in J.P. Newell, *The Book of Creation: An Introduction to Celtic Spirituality* (New Jersey: Paulist Press, 1999).

15. See R. Stalley, *Irish High Crosses* (Dublin: Town House and Country House, 1996), pp. 34-35. See also R. Richardson, and J. Scarry, *An Introduction to Irish High Crosses* (Dublin: Mercier Press, 1986).

16. T. Joyce, *Celtic Christianity*, p. 37.

17. L. Tatman, *An A to Z of Feminist Theology*, p. 238, cited in M. Grey, *The Outrageous Pursuit of Hope: Prophetic Dreams for the Twenty-First Century* (London: Darton, Longman & Todd, 2000).

18. J.P. Newell, *Listening to the Heartbeat of God: An Introduction to Celtic Spirituality* (London/New Jersey: SPCK /Paulist Press, 1997), p. 97.

19. Vatican Council II, *Gaudium et Spes: Pastoral Constitution on the Church in the Modern World*, No. 22.

20. See P. Ricoeur, *History and Truth* (Evanston: Northwesten University, 1965), p. 127.

21. R.E. Guare, *The Arts and Spirituality: Inscapes of Knowing Through Imagination* [online]. Available at http://members.aol.com/jophe00/guare.htm [Accessed 14 May 2004].

22. M. Drumm, and T. Gunning, *A Sacramental People*, Vol. 2 (Dublin: Columba, 2000), p. 16.

23. E. De Waal, *Every Earthly Blessing*, p. 90.

24. P. Tillich, *Systematic Theology*, Vol. 1, p. 166, cited in A. Holton, *A Liberating Spirituality for Religious Educators*, p. 37.

25. W.J. Bausch, *The Yellow Brick Road* (Mystic, Connecticut: Twenty-Third Publications, 1999), p. 119.

26. D.A. Lane, 'Hope: In Need of Retrieval' *The Way* Oct (1999), p. 332.

CLOSING WORD

CHILDREN'S RELIGIOUS EDUCATION

Challenge and Gift

Gareth Byrne

At the Family Mass on Mother's Day the parable of the Prodigal Son was read. The priest asked the young children present what they thought the mother, who isn't mentioned in the story, might have said to her older son, as the feast in honour of his brother's return was celebrated. One six year old gave an instant response:
'Don't you know I will love you always no matter what?'

What more could be said. All the mothers there, all the fathers, the priest and everyone who had gathered to support each other in prayer and worship, paused to allow God's word sink into their hearts:
'Don't you know I will love you always no matter what?'

Religious education draws all those involved – young people, parents, and teachers – into a process that can, at once, be enlightening, holistic, respectful, inclusive and generous. As has been demonstrated already by the writers of articles for this collection, religious education seeks to contribute to the development of the young person, at a personal, human, moral, religious and spiritual level. A dialogue is entered into that seeks to nurture the religious intuition of the child while encouraging the adult to reassess and express in new ways the truths they have come to cherish:

> The child's faith always depends upon his or her own constructions of images and insights. But religious language, rituals and ethical teachings do *awaken* the child to the domain of faith; they channel her or his attention toward the transcendent. They provide experiences of shared attention and celebration of the holy. As such, to use Horace Bushnell's beautiful language, they are 'gifts to the imagination.'[2]

Children are curious about the big questions. Don't we know it! Often it is the actual formulation of the question or the construction of an insight, and not specifically the answer that parents, teachers, religious leaders and others find themselves struggling to provide, which is most significant for the child. Involving children in the re-telling of parables and stories, inviting them to participate in school and parish rituals, teaching them about the moral life, and encouraging them to celebrate God's love for them, day-in-day-out, is a creative and a 'holy' work. Home, parish and school are the natural environments within which primary-level children find support, not only for their everyday physical, emotional and social requirements but also for their everyday religious, moral and spiritual needs.

Home, Parish and School in Partnership

Parents are recognised as the primary educators of their children[3] and as the 'first teachers of their child in the ways of faith.'[4] To affirm this is not to burden parents further but in a sense to set them free – to reassure them that parenting, while at times stretching them to their limits, is centred on all that is true, beautiful, loving and life-giving.

The parish, the Christian faith-community, is a second family within which the young person is nourished and encouraged to feel at home. The parish community, when it flourishes, immerses itself freely and enthusiastically in initiating its young people in Christian love while supporting them in faith and in hope. It provides a space within which to meet and respond to God and neighbour. It offers an invitation to experience the challenge, renewal, fulfilment and joy of the Christian life.

The Education Act of 1998, recognises the school, supported by the State, as a further participant in the religious education of children, providing for 'the moral, spiritual, social and personal development of the child.'[5] Ideally, then, the home, the faith-community to which parent and child belong, and the primary school together form a partnership – a partnership in nurturing the religious development of the child.

According to the survey of primary teachers undertaken by the Irish National Teachers' Organisation in 2002, 51 per cent of teachers questioned, by far the largest response, saw the school as supportive of family and Church in the religious formation of children.[6] Another 21 per cent understood the Church as providing back-up for the school and family in this obligation. In fact, only 7.8 per cent of teachers suggested that schools opt out of partnership in the religious formation of children. Multi-denominational schools, as well as those sponsored by Christian and other faith-communities embrace this responsibility within their stated ethos and in cooperation with parents and local communities of faith. While it is clear that no one religion is given precedence over others in multi-denominational schools, an agreed religious education programme is taught and 'children are encouraged to explore their own religious identities in a safe supportive environment.'[7] It has become apparent that teachers and parents benefit from embracing, extending and developing genuine partnership with each other.[8] One might add that such partnership in the area of religious education does not simply imply teachers collaborating with individual parents and with priests and other local religious leaders. It suggests ongoing, increasing and deepening co-operation between local faith-communities and the school, with committed parents acting as a bridge between the two. In particular, in the Christian context, the sacramental preparation of children can be based on caring collaboration between parish and school. Parents, teachers and parish personnel may find shared responsibility, encouraged by a designated parish catechist, to be the way forward. Such focused engagement, in turn, may suggest further creative partnership between all those involved in the ongoing education of children.

Finding a Response at Home and in the Parish Community
It is evident that many parents of primary-aged children find themselves unsure how best to engage their children in reflecting on their religious faith journey. Martin Kennedy, in his research into primary school religious education, confirms this reality: 'While parents are satisfied with the role of teachers in the religious education of their children, they see little role in this for themselves.'[9] Many do not feel skilled to deal with the questions children ask and may have disengaged from their faith-community and from the religious culture that could support them in their desire to respond positively to their children's religious questions. The reality of drifting

participation within the major Christian churches needs to be recognised while acknowledging that parents are generally keen for their children to be fully initiated in their religious tradition.

Parish communities, too, are acutely aware of the responsibility to educate their young people in a religious understanding of life and love. Parish personnel seem less sure however how best to adapt their role to achieve this in the modern (or even post-modern) world. Ongoing adult religious education, addressing issues such as faith, religious knowing, grace, personal conversion and commitment, seems indispensable. Within many Catholic parishes, Family Mass initiatives, such as the one mentioned at the beginning of this reflection, have given a voice not only to young people, but also to parents, grandparents, neighbours and sometimes teachers within the parish faith-community. The intergenerational aspect of this form of liturgical celebration is as important as the focus on young people. Music and other forms of active participation, such as reading Scripture, leading prayer, and performing liturgical movement and drama, seem to touch into the joyful, though often nervous, openness of children to express what seems important in their relationship with God and their own people. The approach suggested in the introduction to the *Alive-O* series of religious education textbooks used in Catholic schools and echoed in the adaptation of the series, *Follow Me*, developed by the Church of Ireland, Methodist and Presbyterian Boards of Education, captures this joy: 'The task is to live and reach out to others in such a way as to make the gospel attractive.'[10]

The Role of the School in Religious Education

Very often, in fact, it is the school which provides the more structured approach to religious education for the young, based on educational principles, with approved textbooks and resources, under the guidance of teachers who, Kennedy reports are seen as 'capable, confident and committed.'[11] The new Primary Curriculum clearly confirms the position of religious education within a holistic vision of what education can be: 'In seeking to develop the full potential of the individual, the curriculum takes into account the child's affective, aesthetic, spiritual, moral and religious needs.'[12] The religious education envisaged in primary schools, by the State, 'specifically enables the child develop spiritual and moral values and to come to a knowledge of God.'[13] The school is responsible for providing 'religious education consonant with its ethos' while making arrangements for those who do not wish to avail of the particular religious education it offers.[14] With this in mind, the Curriculum document cites the recognition in the Education Act, 1998, of the right of the different major faith traditions to design curricula in religious education at primary level and to supervise their teaching and implementation in the schools they sponsor.[15] Religious education is a whole-school undertaking. The teacher, the chaplain and school leadership support each other within the characteristic spirit of the school, and by their endeavours, develop and build up that spirit.

Acknowledging Children's Religious Development

Two particular religious education needs of children, relevant to their age and stage of development, are worthy of particular attention. Firstly, children are children. They are neither adults nor adolescents. James Fowler, following in the tradition of Piaget, Erikson and Kohlberg, has helped those involved in religious education to capture an understanding of the stages through which faith may develop from childhood through adolescence to adulthood. While such theories are open to critique they can provide a useful foundation upon which to examine educational priorities. In early childhood (from age three to seven), Fowler argues, faith is fantasy-filled and the child is responsive to imaginative interaction with the adults in their lives: 'the child can be powerfully and permanently influenced by examples, moods, actions and stories of the visible faith of primally related adults.'[16] In later childhood (from age eight to twelve approximately) a more linear, narrative construction of coherence and meaning is experienced. A sense is developed of where and with whom the child is at home. This is 'the stage in which the person begins to take on for him- or herself the stories, beliefs and observances that symbolise belonging to his or her community.'[17]

The religious education of primary-school children should therefore focus on helping the child become aware of and grow into the religious community to which they belong while promoting openness and mutual respect for others from a different cultural, ethnic, national or religious background. Within the Christian context teachers of primary-aged school children have always been mandated: 'to foster and deepen the children's faith.'[18] Repeating the stories of their people, a theme addressed by a number of contributors to this volume, and experiencing the language, rituals and ethical teachings of the faith-community with whom they are beginning to identify are appropriate religious education activities for children. Making stars at home to decorate the parish church for Christmas, participating in dramatic presentations of gospel stories on Sunday, saving money at school for children in need, for example, and all the discussions with adults these activities entail, offers children the opportunity to involve themselves personally in religious activities at a level appropriate to their own development.

As J.W. Berryman points out, there is common agreement that the dominant faith development issues during childhood are belonging and being cherished.[19] It is only with the onset of adolescence that young people generally engage more fully in the struggle to find their own identity, looking beyond those who formerly held positions of authority in their lives. Gabriel Moran maintains that the religious educator of children must neither be an indoctrinator nor someone simply holding a discussion. Rather his or her attitude is to communicate to the child in a variety of ways that:

> I and my people are not wrong. My way is not a false way. I know it is true for me because I have experienced it. I am going to show you a world that does exist. I want you to see that world because it is worth seeing. I invite you to join that way.[20]

In affirming such an approach as the appropriate one with children, Moran is clear that only the child in the end can decide to engage in this adventure. The child's freedom not to commit or to raise other issues must always be accepted and respected.

The development in Ireland in the recent past of an increasingly multicultural and multi-faith society means that the primary teacher is challenged to reach out to a variety of individuals and faith-communities, supporting children in coming to appreciate and cherish their own tradition while being hospitable to others, and prompting intercultural dialogue based on respect for each individual's developing religious commitment. What is required is support for children along their respective religious journeys rather than an abstract comparative overview of religions. From the richness of their religious traditions, the 'new Irish' will undoubtedly have something of value to contribute to the Christian way of celebrating life. The Irish Christian tradition, on the other hand, will also offer those of different faiths and cultures new insights in developing their own relationship with God.

Affective, Active and Cognitive Learning

A second issue, relevant to the religious education needs of children, that has been alluded to in any number of ways in this publication, but which can usefully be spelt out further here, is the relationship between affective, active and cognitive learning for children. Often adults with the best of intentions reduce religious education to the intellectual comprehension of religious concepts. Other adults focus almost exclusively on the very real but also limited experience of the child. Religious education curricula should be careful to adopt an integrated approach, drawing together affective opportunity, active engagement, and cognitive reflection, and, thereby, challenging the young person at a variety of complementary learning levels. Heart, hands and head all have their part to play. For the purpose of discussion each of these may be spoken of separately. All three, however, contribute at one and the same time to growth in the child's personal, religious and moral awareness.

Affective learning touches the heart, awakening the person to a deep and personal response to encountered reality. Even the mention of mother or father or God, for instance, will evoke, for most people, an immediate felt response. As leading religious educationalist James Michael Lee indicates, by engaging with emotions, attitudes and values, affective content involves children in becoming aware of their own feeling-reaction and commitment to a given reality.[21] The affective domain is not peripheral to the make-up of humankind. It is a basic disposition, a core orientation of the human person, the gateway to relationship and what we call love. The heart should be given priority in religious education and the child encouraged to trust in this indispensable means of discernment.

Active learning, too, is essential to the growing comprehension of children. It is often by doing that children come to learn what is important for them. For example, educators and parents can teach the meaning of justice by encouraging children's involvement in social action. 'Children learn by doing and mature concepts of justice are more likely when they *do* justice.'[22]

Cognitive or intellectual learning, symbolised by the head, engages the young person in a reflective process central to religious education. Three progressive levels of cognition are generally referred to. According to Lee, they are essential outcomes in religious instruction: knowledge in the limited sense of information (simple apprehension), understanding (grasp of the general principles underlying a given reality) and wisdom (comprehension of the ultimate principles underlying a given reality).[23] While religious knowledge is essential, religious understanding and religious wisdom are more significant, Lee affirms, in helping young people clarify and give an account of their faith. 'Thus it is crucial that the religious educator not simply be satisfied with facilitating knowledge outcomes, but press on and teach understanding and wisdom outcomes as well.'[24]

The synthesis between heart, hands and head is significant for all children. It is particularly important in the light of the contributions in this volume underlining the specific religious education requirements of children with special needs, as well as of those from disadvantaged backgrounds or who are living within distressed family situations. Very often it is by providing varied pathways to learning that the door to a broader, positive and life-giving interpretation of human experience is opened up for young people whatever their situation.

The ongoing attempt in Ireland by the authors of the *Children of God* series and its re-presentation *Alive-O*, to embrace affective, active and cognitive elements in an appropriate manner for childhood learning is clear. The *Alive-O* Teacher's Books are a treasure trove of useful material, far beyond that which is provided in the student's books, highlighting the role of imagination in articulating mystery for the child. The texts and accompanying resources use narrative and symbol to invite the child into relationship with the other person, with the Christian community and with the Ultimate Other, God. Faith is to be understood but it is also to be lived:

> The kind of 'knowing' that we seek is not only one that leads to clarity of thought and articulation, but one that profoundly influences the whole of an individual's approach to life.[25]

The role of the teacher is crucial in making professional decisions as how best to use the material provided in order to facilitate meaning within the particular environmental situation the children inhabit. In today's world, navigating appropriate religious sites on the world wide web, and discerning what is suitable there for children's use, is also a significant issue for teachers and parents. The preparation and training of primary school teachers to deal competently and be at their ease when engaging with religious material in the classroom and with a wide variety of pupil needs is an issue that will always require specific, detailed and ongoing attention and support. The provision, by adults of a safe, positive, imaginative, caring and hope-filled learning environment is essential. Within such, both the child and the adult are free to explore and question, experience and bring forth their own affective potentialities, and by their actions comprehend what is possible and what is true.

Principles for Children's Religious Education
The conversation engaged in, in this book, leads one to suggest that there are specific foundations upon which any valid form of children's religious education, looking to the future should be built. Fundamental principles may be asserted which underpin the authentic religious education of children, at home, in school or in association with the faith community to which they belong.

Children's religious education for the future should seek to:

- Contribute to the revelation and communication of God's love
- Invite the child to respond to God with love and gratitude;
- Respect the child as a human person
- Engage with their personal and social development
- Encourage the child to ask the key questions humankind has always asked
- Cherish the religious tradition of the child
- Foster and deepen the child's faith

- Contribute to the child's religious, spiritual and moral development
- Help the child tell their own story and the story of their faith community
- Promote open, mutually respectful and inclusive attitudes among children of different ethnic and religious backgrounds
- Animate affective, active and cognitive religious experience
- Embrace those with special educational needs
- Facilitate authenticity, commitment and responsibility on the part of the child and the adult working with them
- Breath new life and vitality into the faith-stance, spirituality and religious commitment of the adult participant
- Recognise the whole school, whole community nature of religious education
- Acknowledge its intergenerational character
- Value partnership between home, school and faith community
- Promote hospitality, generosity, compassion, justice, respect, and peace.

Conclusion

The conviction that God loves each and every person, always, no matter what, and that humankind is invited to respond to God's love by 'serving one another in works of love' (Gal 5:13) opens up, as we have seen, a dialogue in faith which suggests that religious education can be both a humanising and an uplifting enterprise, greatly to be valued when it is performed well. Religious education is a challenge but it is also a gift – opening the individual and the community to riches beyond money, power and status. Reflection on themes such as those addressed in this book, discussion within school staff rooms, collaboration with parents and with coordinators of parish and diocesan religious education initiatives, will help, it may be hoped, provide momentum in this area for the future. A growing awareness of partnership in the religious education of children is undoubtedly necessary. A genuine sense of support among parents, teachers and parish personnel, each for the other, is essential as together they investigate new ways of working to provide 'an experience of the love of God flooding through our hearts' (Rom 5:5).

Notes

1. St Gabriel's Parish Family Mass, March 2004. Thank you Maeve.
2. J.W. Fowler, 'Faith and Structuring Meaning', C. Dykstra and S. Parks (eds.) *Faith Development and Fowler* (Birmingham, Alabama: Religious Education Press, 1986), p. 39.
3. See *Bunreacht na hÉireann: Constitution of Ireland* (1937), art. 42:1.
4. *The Rite of Baptism for Children* (Dublin: Catholic Communications Institute of Ireland, 1970), p. 58.
5. See Government of Ireland, *Education Act, 1998* (Dublin: The Stationary Office, 1998), 9(d).
6. See Irish National Teachers' Organisation, *Teaching Religion in the Primary School: Issues and Challenges*, (Dublin: INTO Publications, 2003), p. 53.
7. *Teaching Religion in the Primary School*, p. 33. The particular section cited here is based on information submitted by 'Educate Together'.
8. S. Drudy, 'The Teaching Profession in Ireland: Its Role and Current Challenges' *Studies* 90(2001), p. 373.
9. M. Kennedy, *Islands Apart* (Dublin: Veritas, 2000), p. 3.
10. C. Maloney, F. O'Connell, and B. O'Reilly, *Alive-O 7, Teacher's Book*, (Dublin: Veritas, 2003), p. [25]. For an overview of the entire programme see, for example, the introduction to *Alive-O 7, Teacher's Book*, pp. [5]-[45].
11. M. Kennedy, *Islands Apart*, p. 3.
12. Department of Education and Science, *The Primary School Curriculum: Introduction*, p. 58 [online]. Available at http://www.ncca.ie/bigriver/index.html [Accessed 10 June 2004]. For a useful comparison on this issue with the previous, Department of Education, *Primary School*

Curriculum: Teacher's Handbook, Parts One and Two (Dublin: The Stationary Office, 1971) see K. Williams, 'Pluralism and the Christian Tradition in the New (1999) Primary Curriculum', Religion, Education and the Arts 4 (2003), pp. 30-38.

13. The Primary School Curriculum: Introduction, p. 58.

14. See The Primary School Curriculum: Introduction, p. 58.

15. See The Primary School Curriculum: Introduction, p. 58.

16. J.W. Fowler, Stages of Faith: The Psychology of Human Development and the Quest for Meaning (San Francisco: Harper & Row, 1981), p. 133.

17. J.W. Fowler, Stages of Faith, p. 149.

18. Alive-O 7, Teacher's Book, p. [11].

19. J.W. Berryman 'Faith Development and the Language of Faith', D.E. Ratcliff (ed.) Handbook of Children's Religious Education (Birmingham, Alabama: Religious Education Press, 1992), p. 41.

20. G. Moran, Religious Education Development: Images of the Future (Minneapolis: Winston, 1983), p. 200.

21. See J.M. Lee, The Content of Religious Instruction: A Social Science Approach (Birmingham, Alabama: Religious Education Press, 1985), pp. 197-244.

22. R. Vianello, K. Tamminen and D.E. Ratcliff, 'The Religious Concepts of Children', D.E. Ratcliff (ed.) Handbook of Children's Religious Education, p. 77.

23. See J.M. Lee, The Content of Religious Instruction, pp. 159-183.

24. J.M. Lee, The Content of Religious Instruction, p. 178.

25. Alive-O 7, Teacher's Book, p. [10].

BIBLIOGRAPHY

Abanes, R. *Harry Potter and the Bible: The Menace behind the Magic* (Camp Hill, PA: Horizon Books, 2001).

Armagh Diocesan Biblical Initiative, 28 Sunday July 2002: Ordinary Time: A [online]. Available from: http://www.adbi.net/ [Accessed 14 May 2004].

Bausch, W.J. *A New Look at the Sacraments* (1977), reprinted (Cork: The Mercier Press, 1983).

Bausch, W.J. *The Yellow Brick Road* (Mystic, Connecticut: Twenty-third Publications, 1999).

Bergant, D. 'Come, Let Us Go to the Mountain of the Lord', E. Foley (ed.) *Developmental Disabilities and Sacramental Access: New Paradigm for Sacramental Encounters* (Collegeville, MN: The Liturgical Press, 1994).

Berryman, J.W. 'Teaching as Presence and the Existential Curriculum' in *Religious Education* 85/4 (1990), pp. 509-534.

Berryman, J.W. 'Faith Development and the Language of Faith', D.E. Ratcliff (ed.) *Handbook of Children's Religious Education* (Birmingham, Alabama: Religious Education Press, 1992), pp. 21-55.

Berryman, J.W. *Godly Play: An Imaginative Approach to Religious Education* (1991), reprinted (San Francisco: Harper, 1995), pp. 45-60.

Bradshaw, J. *Homecoming: Reclaiming and Championing your Inner Child* (London: Piatkus Books, 1991).

Bradshaw, J. *Creating Love* (London: Piatkus, 1992).

Bradshaw, J. *The Family: A New Way of Creating Solid Self-Esteem* (Deerfield Beach, Florida: Health Communications, 1996).

Bridger, F. *A Charmed Life: The Spirituality of Potterworld* (London: Darton, Longman & Todd, 2001).

Bunreacht na hÉireann: Constitution of Ireland (1937).

Byrne, G. 'Embracing Life at Its Fullest: Spirituality for Religious Educators and School Chaplains' J. Norman (ed.) *At the Heart of Education: School Chaplaincy and Pastoral Care* (Dublin: Veritas, 2004), pp. 184-196.

Catechism of the Catholic Church (1992), Eng. trans. (Dublin: Veritas, 1994).

Cavalletti, S. *The Religious Potential of the Child* (1979), trans. Missionary Society of St. Paul (New York: Paulist Press, 1983).

Chittister, J. *Wisdom Distilled from the Daily* (San Francisco: Harper & Row, 1991).

Coles, R. *The Spiritual Life of Children* (Boston: Houghton Mifflin, 1990).

Conaty, C. *Including All: Home, School and Community United in Education* (Dublin: Veritas, 2002).

Congregation for the Clergy, *General Directory for Catechesis* (Dublin: Veritas, 1998).

Cooke, B. *Sacraments and Sacramentality* (1983), reprinted (Mystic: Twenty-Third Publications, 1987).

Coghlan, S., Fitzpatrick, M. and O'Dea, L. (eds.) *Changing Faces, Changing Places: A Guide to Multicultural Books for Children* (Dublin: O'Brien Press, 2001).

Creamer, D. 'Finding God in Our Bodies: Theology From the Perspective of People With Disabilities, Part One', *Journal of Religion in Disability and Rehabilitation* 2/1(1995), pp. 27-42.

Crossan, J.D. *The Dark Interval: Towards a Theology of Story*, (Niles, Illinois: Argus, 1975).

Darcy-Berube, F. *Religious Education at a Crossroads: Moving On in the Freedom of the Spirit* (New York: Paulist Press, 1995).

Department of Education, *Primary School Curriculum: Teacher's Handbook, Parts One and Two* (Dublin: The Stationary Office, 1971).

Department of Education, *Charting our Education Future: White Paper on Education* (Dublin: The Stationary Office, 1995).

Department of Education and Science, *Primary School Curriculum: Introduction* (Dublin: The Stationary Office, 1999). Also available at http://www.ncca.ie/bigriver/index.html [Accessed 10 June 2004].

Department of Education and Science, *Primary School Curriculum: SPHE Teacher Guidelines* (Dublin, The Stationary Office, 1999).

Department of Education and Science, *Information Booklet on Asylum Seekers, 2001.*

De Waal, E. *Every Earthly Blessing: Rediscovering the Celtic Tradition* (1991), reprinted (Harrisbourg PA: Moorehouse Publishing, 1999).

Dewey, J. 'My Pedagogic Creed', M.S. Dworkin (ed.) *Dewey in Education*, Classics in Education 3 (New York: Teacher's College, Columbia University, 1971).

Drudy, S. 'The Teaching Profession in Ireland: Its Role and Current Challenges' *Studies* 90(2001), pp. 363-375.

Drumm, M. *Passage to Pasch* (Dublin: Columba, 1998).

Drumm, M. and Gunning, T. *A Sacramental People,* Vol. 1 (Dublin: Columba, 1999).

Drumm, M. and Gunning, T. *A Sacramental People*, Vol. 2 (Dublin: Columba, 2000).

Edwards, J. *Sharing Our Faith: Involving People with Learning and Communication Difficulties in the Spiritual Life of the Parish Community* (Essex: Matthew James Publishing, 1997).

Eisland, N. *The Disabled God: Towards a Liberatory Theology of Disability* (Nashville: Abingdon Press, 1994).

Erricker, C., Erriker, J. et al, *The Education of the Whole Child* (London: Cassell, 1997).

Fowler, J.W. 'Faith and the Structuring of Meaning', C. Brusselmans (ed.) *Toward Moral and Religious Maturity: The First International Conference on Moral and Religious Development* (Morristown: Silver Burdett Company, 1980).

Fowler, J.W. *Stages of Faith: The Psychology of Human Development and the Quest for Meaning* (San Francisco: Harper & Row, 1981).

Fowler, J.W. 'Faith and Structuring Meaning', C. Dykstra and S. Parks (eds.) *Faith Development and Fowler* (Birmingham, Alabama: Religious Education Press, 1986).

Fowler, J.W., 'The Vocation of Faith Development Theory', J.W. Fowler, K.E. Nipkow and F. Schweitzer (eds.) *Stages of Faith and Religious Development: Implications for Church, Education and Society* (Centre for Research in Faith and Moral Development, Candler School of Theology, Emory University: SCM Press, 1991).

Freud, S. 'The Passion and Challenge of Teaching', M. Okazawa, R.J. Anderson and R. Traver (eds.) *Teachers, Teaching and Teacher Education* (Cambridge, MA: Harvard University Press, 1987).

Government of Ireland, *Education Act, 1998* (Dublin: The Stationary Office, 1998).

Groome, T.H. *Sharing Faith: A Comprehensive Approach to Religious Education and Pastoral Ministry – The Way of Shared Praxis* (Eugene, Oregon: Wipf and Stock, 1998).

Groome, T.H. *Educating For Life: A Spiritual Vision for Every Teacher and Parent* (1998), paperback edition (New York: Crossroad, 2001).

Groome, T.H. 'Forging in the Smithy of the Teacher's Soul', N. Prendergast and L. Monahan (eds.) *Reimagining the Catholic School* (Dublin: Veritas, 2003), pp. 35-45.

Guare, R.E. *The Arts and Spirituality: Inscapes of Knowing Through Imagination* [online]. Available at: http://members.aol.com/jophe00/guare.htm [Accessed 14 May 2004].

Guzie, T. *The Book of Sacramental Basics* (New York: Paulist Press, 1981).

Hall, S. *Into the Christian Community* (Washington DC: National Catholic Educational Association, 1982).

Harrington, M.T. 'Affectivity and Symbol in the Process of Catechesis' in E. Foley (ed.) *Developmental Disabilities and Sacramental Access: New Paradigms for Sacramental Encounters* (Collegeville, MN: The Liturgical Press, 1994), pp. 53-72.

Harrington, W.J. *John: Spiritual Theologian – The Jesus of John,* (Dublin: Columba, 1999).

Hay, D. with Nye, R. *The Spirit of the Child* (London: Harper Collins Religious, 1998).

Hederman, M.P. *The Haunted Inkwell: Art and Our Future,* (Dublin: Columba, 2001).

Holland, J. and Henriot, P. *Social Analysis: Linking Faith and Justice* (New York: Orbis Books, 1995).

Holton, A. *A Liberating Spirituality for Religious Educators* (Lima, Ohio: Wyndham Hall Press, 2002).

Houghton, J. *A Closer Look at Harry Potter: Bending and Shaping the Minds of Our Children* (Eastbourne: Kingsway, 2001).

http://www.bomis.com/rings/Nharry_potter_series-articles_and_interviews-art [Accessed 29 June 2004].

http://www.scholastic.com/harrypotter/author [Accessed 29 June 2004].

Hunt, J. 'Ten Reasons Not to Hit Your Kids', Appendix, A. Miller, *Breaking Down the Walls of Silence to Join the Waiting Child* (London: Virago, 1992).

Information Leaflet for Parents of Asylum Seeker and Refugee Children attending Primary Education, prepared by the Reception and Integration Agency (August 2001).

Irish Episcopal Commission on Catechetics, *Alive-O* (Dublin: Veritas, 1996-2004).

Irish National Teachers' Organisation, *The Challenge of Diversity: Education Support for Ethnic Minority Children* (Dublin: INTO Publications, 1998).

Irish National Teachers' Organistion, *Intercultural Guidelines for Schools,* (Dublin: INTO Publications, 2002).

Irish National Teachers' Organisation, *Teaching Religion in the Primary School: Issues and Challenges,* (Dublin: INTO Publications, 2003).

John Paul II, *Catechesi Tradendae,* Eng. trans. (Middlegreen: St. Paul Publications, 1979).

John Paul II, *Homily at Norcia,* 23rd March, 1980. Available from: http://www.vatican.va/holy_father/john_paul_ii/speeches/1980/march/ [Accessed 27 May 2004].

John Paul II, *Novo Millennio Ineunte,* Eng. trans. (2001) [online]. Available from: http://www.vatican.va/holy_father/john_paul_ii/index.htm [Accessed 10 May 2004].

Joyce, T. *Celtic Christianity: A Sacred Tradition, A Vision of Hope* (New York: Orbis Books, 1998).

Kakkioniemi, A. 'Church and Social Integration of Disabled People', *Panorama: International Journal of Comparative Religious Education and Values* 13/1(2001).

Kasper, W. 'Church as Communio', *Communio: International Catholic Review* 13(1986), pp. 100-117.

Kavanagh, A. 'Initiation: Baptism and Confirmation', M.J. Taylor (ed.) *The Sacraments: Readings in Contemporary Sacramental Theology* (New York: Alba House, 1981).

Kavanagh, A. *Confirmation: Origins and Reform* (New York: Pueblo, 1988).

Kearney, R. *On Stories* (London: Routledge, 2002).

Kennedy, M. *Islands Apart* (Dublin: Veritas, 2000).

Klein, C. *The Myth of the Always Happy Child* (New York: Harper & Row, 1975).

Kohlberg, L. *Essays on Moral Development,* Vol. 1 (San Francisco: Harper & Row, 1981).

Lane, D.A. 'Hope: In Need of Retrieval' *The Way* Oct (1999).

Lee, J.M. *The Content of Religious Instruction: A Social Science Approach* (Birmingham, Alabama: Religious Education Press, 1985).

Leijssen, L. 'Confirmation in Context', *Louvain Studies* 20 (1995).

Liebschner, J. *Foundations of Progressive Education: The History of the National Froebel Society* (Cambridge: Lutterworth Press, 1991).

Liebschner, J. *A Child's Work: Freedom and Play in Froebel's Educational Theory and Practice* (Cambridge: Lutterworth Press, 2001).

Lewis, C.S. 'On Stories' Walter Hooper (ed.) *Of This and Other Worlds* (London: Fount Paperbacks, 1982).

Lilley, I. *Friedrich Froebel: A Selection from His Writings* (Cambridge University Press, 1967).

Lonergan, B. 'A Post-Hegelian Philosophy of Religion' in F.E. Crowe (ed.) *A Third Collection* (New York: Paulist Press, 1985).

Martin, D. 26 April 2004 [online]. Available from: www.dublindiocese.ie [Accessed 23 June 2004].

Martin, M. *Discipline in Schools: Report to the Minister for Education, Niamh Bhreathnach*, Spring 1997.

McCormack, B., Rafferty, M. and Lynch C. *Values to Practice: A Practical Course in Normalisation for Front Line Staff* (Dublin: Open Road, St Michael's House Training, 1990).

Miller, A. *Pictures of a Childhood* (London: Virago, 1995).

Moran, G. *Religious Education Development: Images of the Future* (Minneapolis: Winston, 1983).

Neal, C. *The Gospel According to Harry Potter* (Louisville, Kentucky: John Knox Press, 2001).

Neal, C. *What's a Christian to Do with Harry Potter?* (New York: Waterbrook Press, 2001).

Nodding, N. *Caring: A Feminine Approach to Ethics and Moral Education* (Berkley: University of California Press, 1984).

O'Donnell, D. 'My Hopes for My Church', *The Tablet* 15th February 2003, p. 2.

Ó hÓgáin, D. *The Sacred Isle: Belief and Religion in Pre-Christian Ireland* (Cork: Collins Press, 1999).

Ó Laoghaire, D. 'Celtic Spirituality', C. Jones, G. Wainwright, and E. Yarnold (eds.) *The Study of Spirituality* (London: SPCK, 1986).

Palmer, P. *To Know as We Are Known: A Spirituality of Education* (San Francisco: Harper & Row, 1983).

Palmer, P. *The Courage to Teach* (San Francisco: Jossey-Bass, 1998).

Palmer, P. 'Evoking the Spirit in Public Education', *Educational Leadership* 56/4 (1999).

Paul VI, *Evangelii Nuntiandi,* Eng. trans. (Dublin: Veritas, 1975).

Power, D.N. 'Households of Faith in the Coming Church', M.Warren (ed.) *Source Book for Modern Catechetics,* Vol. 2 (Winona, MN: St Mary's Press, 1987).

Quinn, F. 'Confirmation: Does it Make Sense', *Ecclesia Orans* (1988).

Ricoeur, P. 'Listening to the Parables of Jesus', C.E. Reagan and D. Stewart (eds.) *The Philosophy of Paul Ricoeur: An Anthology of His Work* (Boston: Beacon Press, 1978).

Robinson, E. *The Original Vision* (Oxford: The Religious Experience Research Unit, Manchester College, 1977).

Rogers, B. *Behaviour Management: A Whole-School Approach* (London: Paul Chapman Publishing, 2000).

Sacred Congregation for Divine Worship, *Directory on Children's Masses* (London: Catholic Truth Society, 1974).

Schillebeeckx, E. *The Church with a Human Face: A New and Expanded Theology of Ministry,* trans. J. Bowden (London: SCM, 1985).

Schneiders, S. 'Spirituality in the Academy' *Theological Studies* 50/2(1989), pp. 676-697.

Searle, M. *Christening: The Making of Christians* (Collegeville, MN: Liturgical Press, 1980).

Smith, A. *Discipline for Learning: A Positive Approach to Teaching and Learning Manual,* unpublished.

'The New Irish', *The Irish Times,* 9–19 May 2004.

The Rite of Baptism for Children (Dublin: Catholic Communications Institute of Ireland, 1970).

Treston, K. *Paths and Stories: Spirituality for Teachers and Catechists* (Dublin: Veritas, 1991).

Turner, P. *The Baby in Solomon's Court* (New York: Paulist, 1993).

Vanier, J. *Eruption to Hope* (New York: Paulist Press, 1971).

Vanier, J. *Our Journey Home: Rediscovering a Common Humanity Beyond Our Differences* (London: Hodder & Stoughton, 1997).

Vatican Council II, *Gaudium et Spes: Pastoral Constitution on the Church in the Modern World*, edited by A. Flannery (New York: Costello Publishing, 1977).

Vianello, R., Tamminen, K. and Ratcliff, D.E. 'The Religious Concepts of Children', D.E. Ratcliff (ed.) *Handbook of Children's Religious Education* (Birmingham, Alabama: Religious Education Press, 1992), pp. 56-81.

Wadell, P.J. 'Pondering the Anomaly of God's Love: Ethical Reflections on Access to the Sacraments' in E. Foley (ed.) *Developmental Disabilities and Sacramental Access: New Paradigms for Sacramental Encounters* (Collegeville, MN: The Liturgical Press, 1994).

Webb-Mitchell, B. *Unexpected Guests at God's Banquet: Welcoming People with Disabilities Into the Church* (New York: Crossroad, 1994).

Williams, K. 'Pluralism and the Christian Tradition in the New (1999) Primary Curriculum', *Religion, Education and the Arts* 4 (2003), pp. 30-38.

Yucker, H.E. *Attitudes Towards Persons with Disabilities* (New York: Springer Publishing, 1980).